INTERNATIONAL TRAVEL SECRETS

TAKE SHORTER TRIPS, MORE OFTEN, FOR LESS.

MICHAEL WEDAA

International Travel Secrets

Copyright © 2020 Michael Wedaa

All rights reserved.

ISBN: 978-1-7360629-0-6 (print)

ISBN: 978-1-7360629-2-0 (ebook)

This book is dedicated to the following individuals:

Michael Tran

For inviting me to join the group in Vietnam for New Year's—the trip that was the catalyst for most of my travel adventures, and for picking up your phone in a Mexican restaurant located in Nha Trang that is owned by a Native American who lives in France.

Lew Valle (or is it Valle Vega?)

For joining Team No Sleep in an around-the-world-trip that ended with my passing out defiantly in a hotel lobby in Ulaanbaatar, and for creating our own translation for "Turno!"

David Sariñana

For always saying "yes" even though you do not yet know the itinerary, and for your deep sympathy for my broken toothbrush in Hanoi. Here's to the death trip!

Congratulations! You've just gotten access to tips and secrets that will save you hundreds or even thousands of dollars over your lifetime. To thank you for purchasing this book, I am giving away some FREE travel tools that will help make your next travel adventure even better.

Go to https://www.internationaltravelsecrets.com/travel-tools. There you will find FREE resources such as these:

- Best travel credit cards
- Layover planning checklist
- Best and worst airlines
- Travel packing list
- Links to helpful visa and entry requirement sites
- Quiz: which region of the world fits your personality?

And much more!

Happy traveling!

Table Of Contents

CHAPTER 1

DEBUNKING TRAVEL MYTHS

"I'll never be able to do that," is what I told myself whenever I saw one of my friends or someone on TV hiking through the mountains of Machu Picchu or some other exotic destination around the world. Like most Americans, I, too, bought into the myth that international travel had to be long, painstakingly planned, and expensive. As a child, I began by traveling around the US with my family. We would pack up the car and hit stops such as Sequoia or the Grand Canyon—wherever the best camping spots were. However, my first international trip did not occur until I was twenty-eight when a friend invited me to visit Europe.

We visited Greece, Italy, Spain, and the Netherlands. My friend did all the planning, and I just showed up. My next trip happened the following year as the same friend organized a trip to Brazil, Argentina, and Peru. I did not travel internationally again until six or seven years later when twenty of my friends decided to go to Vietnam for New Year's. When I arrived in this strange, new place, I awakened to a new reality: I was bitten by the travel bug and began planning trips on my own.

Up until this point, I had never had the impetus to sit down, plan a trip, and convince friends to go with me. I am fortunate enough to have had these initial travel invitations from friends, without which I would not be where I am today, having seen more than half of the countries on the globe.

Unfortunately, many of us fall into the same trap that I did: thinking that international travel is not possible for us or that it is reserved for the wealthy or extremely adventurous. We have succumbed to a number of travel myths when it comes to leaving the country. It turns out that this is uniquely an American cultural anomaly.

While out and about, it is common to find numerous travelers from Europe, Asia, and Australia. Traveling to other countries is a staple in these cultures and part of this phenomenon stems from the fact that it is common in many countries for workers to have a mandated six to eight weeks of paid vacation. International travel to these people becomes all but a requirement as does learning multiple languages. It is common to meet Europeans who speak up to six languages or more. So let's debunk the myths we, as a nation, have subscribed to that keep us near home:

1. Traveling internationally is dangerous

Most countries I have traveled to are safe. I have rarely felt uncomfortable or insecure when traveling—even if it is off the beaten path. A combination of research and common sense will help you avoid any unwanted incidents. Pay attention to your surroundings. Even in our home cities, we have dark alleys we avoid at night. Use this same common sense when you are traveling. Yes, some areas of the world will require you to use increased caution when visiting. (In the safety tips and secrets chapter, you will learn how to use the US Department of State website as a tool for the latest danger level and news listed by country. You will also find other helpful safety tips later in this book.)

2. It has to be expensive

I know people that have purchased all-inclusive tours to Europe for $10,000 or $15,000 per person. That is fine if you prefer your entire trip planned for you or you have the bank account balance to support it. However, a short international trip can cost less than $1,000 if you follow the tips in this book. That's right . . . less than $1,000 including flight, hotel, and food. The most expensive parts of a trip are the flights and hotels. Once you get those out of the way, you can choose how much you want to spend trying local food or booking local experiences.

Luckily, you can find many ways to travel cheaper than you ever thought possible—and the good news is that you can choose to employ all the tactics in this book and travel on a student budget. If you have a little more money to play with, you can pick and choose the tactics that fit best with your budget and invest a little more into luxuries you are not willing to sacrifice in exchange for a low price. For instance, I am willing to forego first or business class in lieu of a much cheaper airfare. And I don't need a luxurious hotel. I once stayed in a hotel in Nepal that had no elevator (we were on the sixth floor) and even had a hole in the wall from the bathroom to the outside. While I am willing to scrimp on flights and hotels, I am not willing to sacrifice the quality of food, wine, or cigars in order to save a few bucks. That is my travel preference. We each have our own list of must-haves and not-so-necessary to have, so pick and choose cafeteria style which techniques in this book work best for your travel preferences. There is no one correct way to travel.

3. You have to travel for two weeks or longer

Many people subscribe to the idea that in order to make an international trip worth the effort of a long flight, it has to last two or more weeks. Nothing could be further from the truth. Of course, all our situations are different. Some have the flexibility to stay in one place for many months at a time while others may only have the budget and the time off from work for a five-day trip. (Check out my two-day stay chapter and learn how to get the necessary time off work using weekends plus a few sick days or vacation days to spend just five days in another continent if that is all time allows. Include both weekends to make it nine days, thereby only taking five actual workdays off.) Do not be afraid to push past the norms when it comes to traveling. You will find that all you have learned about travel may not always work to the best of your advantage.

4. You have to stay in the airport on a layover

Many are afraid to leave the airport on a layover. Some even stay in a hotel connected to the airport because they are so afraid of missing their flights. Do not be afraid to go against the grain on this one. A layover can be an excellent addition to your itinerary if you manage your time wisely when you choose to venture out into the city. I have experienced many countries while on a layover, and best of all, the stop is *free*; it is already included in the cost of your flight. A little research into how far the airport is from the city center and the cheapest and quickest way to travel back and forth can assist you in avoiding missing your connecting flight. I have used trains, taxis, and even Uber when available. Choose whichever fits both your budget of money and time. Start stacking up your list of countries visited by using the tips in the Using Layovers as a Tool chapter

None of these myths are true, and later I will show you how to get around all of them. The reality is that anyone can travel the world cheaply and with ease. This was not necessarily true twenty-five years ago pre-internet. At that time you had to hire a travel agent to do all the heavy lifting and pay the agent a fee on top of an already pricey itinerary. Nowadays you can look online to see whether or not you need a visa, whether a taxi is better than a train, what hotels look like both inside and outside, what neighborhoods are safe, where to change currency, how other travelers rate a particular tour, etc.

If you are willing to break beyond your comfort zone, travel can be a great way to rediscover yourself and put a face to the history you learned in school (and some that you did not). You will see both the world and your home in a different light, try new foods, make new friends, have long or short-term relationships . . . anything you want.

The biggest question people ask me is "How do you do it?" That's what I will show you in this book. But just know that you get to find your own travel style. You may have heard the story of a lady who always cut the end off the ham before she put it in the oven. When her daughter questioned her odd practice, she replied that was how her mom always cooked her hams, and she had cooked her hams that way since she moved out of her mother's house years ago. Her daughter eventually called her grandmother to ask why it was necessary to cut the end off the ham. Her grandmother deferred to the great grandmother as the great grandmother always did the same. Upon asking her great grandmother why it was necessary to cut the end off the ham before cooking it, the great grandmother revealed that she had to in order to fit it into the one pan she had. They were poor and could not afford a larger pan at the time, so an unnecessary habit was created that lasted two more generations.

My parents used to take us on camping trips when we were young. We used to get up at 4 a.m. to pack the car to get on the road early. My parents hated starting a long trip on such lack of sleep but chose to do it that way simply because that's what their parents did. At some point, they came to the realization that they did not have to leave the house before the sun came up. We then changed the habit and instead got on the road near

10 a.m., well-rested and eager to see what was in store for us.

The point of these stories is that you have to find your *own* travel style. Do not base it on what your friends, parents, the media, or even what this book tells you. Take a trip and try a few new ways of doing things to see what works for you. Do not let anyone else dictate how you enjoy your world of exploration. You do you.

CHAPTER 2

FLIGHT BOOKING SECRETS

Flights . . . the single biggest expense of any trip
overseas or anywhere for that matter. Let's discuss how
to avoid overpaying for flights. In this chapter I will be
sharing not only the best times to fly but also provide
never-before-heard secrets that can save you 80 percent
or more on flights to your favorite destinations. The
first step for sidestepping high airfares is to avoid travel
during the summer or during the holidays. While it is
possible to use the methods that follow to find deals
even during the busy times listed above, I prefer to
travel during the spring or fall. Not only is the weather
milder in many locations throughout the world but
the places you visit are much less crowded during
these months, allowing for a more pleasant travel
experience. I do occasionally travel during the winter
months to destinations that either have good weather all
year round, such as the Mediterranean or the Caribbean,
or in places south of the equator that have opposite
seasons.

ITA Matrix

Timing is not the only means of obtaining cheaper
flights. The best tool to use for finding deeply
discounted flights originates from a site called ITA
Matrix (https://matrix.itasoftware.com/). Developed by
MIT engineers, ITA Matrix helps you find the cheapest
day to fly to a particular destination, but that is not

what makes this site unique. The site offers impressive filtering functions under "Advanced Controls" that no other flight search tools offer. You can dictate where you would like to have a layover or even which layover stops to leave out of the search results. You can also choose to have the results offer one specific airline or exclude specific airlines among many other details. While you cannot book directly from the site, you can see if leaving a day or two earlier could save you as much as 50 percent or more. Once you find the information you need, you have to go to a travel website or the airline website to book the flight. Google eventually bought the site and merged the technology into Google Flights—the best travel tool I have found to date. While ITA Matrix still offers a way to better filter preferences, Google Flights is a bit more user friendly and has a few features that I prefer.

Google Flights

Google Flights not only allows you to see what days are the cheapest to fly and what site has the cheapest fares but also allows you to purchase tickets by following the links provided on the site. Sometimes you will purchase directly from the airline, and sometimes it will direct you to sites such as Priceline or Expedia.

So how do you use the functions of Google Flights to book flights as low as $128 to get from Los Angeles to Europe? Yes, I did that. If you already know where you would like to go and when, grab your laptop or jump on your desktop computer. **Note: Google Flights does NOT offer all of the advanced functions on the mobile app, mobile browsers, or on most tablets.**

If you already know where you want to go:

1. Go to Google Flights (www.google.com/flights) and type in your desired destination.
2. Click on "Round Trip" in the upper left-hand corner and change it to "One Way."

3. Now click on the date and a calendar will pop up. In a few seconds, the prices will load on each day of the month and this will show you the cheapest days to leave. (The prices that show up in green indicate the cheaper days to fly.)

4. The arrow on the right of the calendar will allow you to advance the months to future dates.

For a detailed video on how to use this method to book cheap flights, visit https://www.internationaltravelsecrets.com/online-courses.

As I write this, I see that flying from Los Angeles to Paris will cost me $1,062 if I leave on the 4th of January. However, if I wait until the 20th, the flight costs only $188, saving me 83 percent.

What if you are not sure where you want to go? Not to worry. What if I told you that you could look at a map of cities with specific airfare indicated next to them in order to help you choose the location of your next adventure? The best way to find cheap flights when you do not know exactly which city you want to visit is to use the map function on Google Flights.

If you are not sure where you want to go:

1. **Start over on a new page** and go to Google Flights (www.google.com/flights)

2. Click on "Round Trip" in the upper left-hand corner and change it to "One Way."

3. Leave the destination blank and click on the map located below the date field.

4. You will see a map of your home country appear with the cheapest fares to different cities.

5. Zoom out to find the continent you are interested in visiting.

6. When you see a price that appeals to you on the map, click on it to see what date that fare applies.

7. The date will appear to the left of the map along with applicable flight information. These flights will all be within six months of today's date.

8. If you know what month you would like to travel, click on the calendar symbol in the upper left-hand corner where it says, "trip in the next six months."

9. It will list the upcoming months individually.

10. Click on the month that works for you and click "done" in the lower right-hand corner.

11. Zoom out on the map to find a list of fares in the continent you wish to visit.

For a detailed video on how to use this method to book cheap flights, visit https://www.internationaltravelsecrets.com/online-courses.

Right now using this tool, I see a flight from Los Angeles to London for $160 and to Barcelona for $170. For those of you with a stomach for adventure, you can travel to Colombia for $137, Morocco for $243, or Indonesia for $264. These are just what I see while casually looking as I write in this text. If I took the time to really dig in, I may be able to find even cheaper flights to those destinations.

One great part about traveling is once you have flown into a particular region, the flights are ultra-cheap to get to other cities or other countries within the same region (see below for saving money on fares by creating a faux layover). Once you get to Europe, for example, flights can be as low as $28 from Paris to Barcelona or from London to Prague. Once you get to Asia, flights can be as low as $39 from Singapore to Malaysia or $56 from Singapore to the Philippines. I do not know how airlines can make a profit with such low fares, but I'll let them worry about that.

One problem people encounter is finding that a

particular destination has a daunting fare—even when they use the steps mentioned above. If that is the case, try adding what I call a faux layover. A faux layover is a layover that you create in order to save money. If you take a flight to one of the major airport hubs in the world, you can catch a cheap flight to destinations that may be rare from your home city but more common from a regional airport hub. Major hubs around the world include London, Paris, Rome, Barcelona, Istanbul, Dubai, Singapore, Shanghai, and Beijing to name a few. If the airfare to your desired destination is too expensive, try flying to a major regional airport hub first, then check the prices from the regional hub to your destination. For example, I wanted to visit Prague, but the flights were well over $900. So I flew to Norway for $128 and caught a flight to Prague for $45, effectively saving over $700 . . . and I got to check out Oslo, Norway, for a day.

If you prefer to get on to your intended destination as quickly as possible, you can book a flight that departs from the regional hub a few hours after you arrive. This technique requires you to go through customs and pick up your luggage in order to recheck it, so be sure to allow enough time (at least two hours is recommended, but I have done it with less time available). You just created a faux layover and saved hundreds of dollars in doing so!

Some of you may prefer to check out the city that houses the airport of the regional hub for a few hours longer . . . maybe even overnight. This is a great way to simply experience a local restaurant and a historical landmark or two. If you choose to spend several hours on this layover, you may have time for a quick organized tour before flying out to your intended destination. Take a look at the next chapter for more details on how to make the most out of a layover.

CHAPTER 3

USING LAYOVERS AS A TOOL

So many travelers have condemned themselves to rotting in the airport for five or ten hours while waiting for their international connections, or they waste time in an airport hotel, thinking that a bed or TV will help the time pass more quickly. I choose to use my layovers as a bonus stop—a *free* pass to see an additional city or country on my way to a planned destination.

If you have a full day or overnight layover, try experiencing the city. You have many options to explore. I have done everything from simply enjoying a beer at a local pub on my own all the way to taking a tour of the Great Wall of China before heading back to the airport. On an overnight layover in Rome, I had delicious food and wine at a restaurant before having a late-night visit at Trevi Fountain and the Pantheon. In the morning, I took a brief tour of the Vatican, which included the Sistine Chapel before heading back to the airport. Recently, I had an overnight layover in Athens and had some amazing Greek food while watching patrons participate in Greek Dance. I marveled at some brightly lit ruins on my way to smoking some hookah at a late-night lounge. In the morning, I took some pictures at the Acropolis before catching a cab to the airport.

Your exploration can be simple: try the local food, check out a few historical sites, or just simply hang out at a cafe to take the city in as brief as it may be. If you would like a more organized experience, try taking a tour if you have enough time; it can be as long or short as you want. Sometimes you will have enough time for a group tour, and in other situations, you may want to pay for a tailored private tour that includes transportation to and from the airport.

Most major cities in the world offer a hop-on, hop-off bus tour that stops by most of the major sights and landmarks in a particular location. Headphones are offered for pre-recorded information about each stop in eight different languages. These tours are a great way to see a city in a short amount of time on a layover. You can choose to stay at each attraction for a quick photo before you hop back on the bus or spend some time exploring and take the next bus once you are satisfied. If you have a shorter layover and do not have time to ride the bus for the entire loop, you can take a taxi to the airport from any point during the hop-on, hop-off bus loop according to your flight schedule demands.

Besides experiencing a new culture for a few hours, taking advantage of your layover also allows you to decide if the city is worth coming back or not. It's a lot like wine tasting—if you like what you see, you buy the bottle. If not, you pour out your glass and move on to the next stop.

Remember to keep careful track of time if you choose to leave the airport on a layover. You must budget time to go through customs and verify in advance whether or not you need a visa to enter the country in which you have just landed. Nothing is more frustrating than the added time and expense of missing a flight, whether it be on a layover, at a planned destination, or on your way home. So be sure to research how much time it takes to get to the city center and back by taxi, bus, train, or whatever form of transportation you choose. When time is tight, I prefer to use the more direct, yet more expensive choice of a taxi or Uber. There is no hassle with overshooting your train stop and the drivers usually know the best routes to the airport. If you do your research and manage your time properly, you have just added another stop to your itinerary . . . for free!

Go to https://www.internationaltravelsecrets.com/travel-tools for a free layover planning checklist.

A lot of people accuse me of being crazy or complain that four, eight, or twelve hours is not enough time to experience a city, but where is it written that you must spend two weeks in order to enjoy your time in any given country? No one says you must experience every corner of a city or country in one trip. If that is the way you choose to do it, please feel free. We all need to travel in a manner that fits our unique interests best. However, this book is for those of you looking to find new, maybe better, and cheaper ways of seeing what the world has to offer. Picture it as going to a buffet. You place samples of what looks good on your plate and try them. When you return, you fill up only on the food items that you enjoyed most.

CHAPTER 4

THE TWO-DAY STAY

For those of you who are traveling on a budget or cannot get extended time off work, consider the two-day stay in each city. I created the two-day stay to maximize the number of cities or countries I can visit on a trip. This method allows me an opportunity to see a city and/or its surroundings without spending the typical two-week vacation there. On day one, I take an organized tour, and on day two, I casually explore the city on my own.

After researching what I find to be the most interesting landmarks in a desired destination, I book a tour for the first day that covers the majority of these landmarks. This enables me to get the lay of the land in a particular city. Tour guides offer a wealth of information, not just about the sights and landmarks but also about local cuisine and nightlife. Then, on the second day, I can revisit the places I enjoyed from the tour or go somewhere entirely new. This is a good time to lie on the beach or try hidden gem restaurants that only the locals know about. I enjoy sitting in a corner cafe watching the world go by on a cobblestone street. This two-day stay allows you to see the more famous historical landmarks while taking in the culture and beating heart of a city, albeit through a brief snapshot.

If time and budget allow, try taking the modified three-day-stay approach. This one mirrors the two-day stay outlined above but allows for an extra day to take a day trip outside of the city. Here is an example of a trip I planned in Ljubljana, Slovenia:

- Day one: 2.5-hour city tour that includes most of the cultural and historical sites inside the city limits.
- Day two: 10-hour tour that includes a stop at Lake Bled, Predjama Castle, and Postojna Cave.
- Day three: Relax in the city to visit restaurants, neighborhood cafes, and bars in historical buildings.

The three-day stay allows you to get a more in-depth view of a country by checking out a region outside of your chosen arrival city in a particular country. Many of you will balk at this approach, but every single person that has traveled with me so far has become a believer and loves this method of exploring the world on a budget without taking long leaves of absence.

As a bonus, you won't spend a lot of money only to find out that a certain destination does not have that much to offer, and you wish you had only planned a few days there. That has happened to me on a few occasions. One such time was during a trip to Tajikistan. We simply booked too many days in Khujand as it doesn't have a lot to see—even TripAdvisor lists only ten sights and landmarks. We stayed here a few days too long and simply rotted until our flight to Uzbekistan. Although we had the best street kebabs I have ever eaten in my life, I could have saved money and spent time in a location with more to see and do.

As I mentioned before, each person has his or her own preferred style of travel—and there is no right or wrong. However, I recommend you try this method at least once. It is a great way to see more of the world in small snippets. Remember that you can always return to cities and countries you enjoyed at a later date and spend more time there. I have returned many times to Istanbul, Paris, Madrid, Baku, Prague, and many more.

CHAPTER 5

TOUR BOOKING SECRETS

Use TripAdvisor for booking tours. TripAdvisor's site (or app) is a useful tool for finding hotels and restaurants, but I use it most for filtering landmarks I want to visit and tours I want to experience. On the site or in the app, you can enter your destination and look for attractions that interest you in that particular location. In order to find the right tour, you have to decide which tours include the landmarks you wish to see. This will take a little time and research, but it pays to know which attractions you would like to visit before committing to a tour. Here is how you use the app to find the attractions that may appeal to you:

On the TripAdvisor Mobile App

1. Type in the name of the city you will be visiting.
2. A list of matching cities will pop up. Click on the correct city.
3. Click on "Things to Do."
4. The bottom row will say "Top Attractions" on the left.
5. Click on "See all" on the bottom right.
6. The attractions will appear in order of popularity.
7. If you wish to narrow the results, click on "Filter" at the bottom middle of the screen.

8. Click on "Attraction Category," and filter the results with the following options:

- Boat Tours & Water Sports
- Fun & Games
- Nature & Parks
- Sights & Landmarks
- Food & Drink
- Concerts & Shows
- Transportation
- Shopping
- Zoos & Aquariums
- Museums
- Traveler Resources
- Outdoor Activities
- Spas & Wellness
- Events
- Classes & Workshops
- Water & Amusement Parks
- Tours
- Nightlife
- Casinos & Gambling

On the TripAdvisor website

1. Type in the name of the city you will be visiting.

2. A list of matching cities will pop up. Click on the correct city.

3. Click on "things to do."

4. Click on "Attractions" toward the center of the screen.

5. The attractions will appear in order of popularity.

6. If you wish to narrow the results, notice the "Types of Attractions" on the left side of the screen.

7. Check the appropriate attraction category to filter the results.

Once you select a landmark, you can learn more about it. Other tourists have uploaded their pictures of each of the landmarks, so I scroll through the pictures of each landmark to determine whether or not I want to visit it. I also read the reviews from other travelers to see if I need to be aware of any pluses or minuses. Sometimes I will decide to pass on a landmark if too many of the reviews indicate there is not much to see.

Once I compile a list of the landmarks of interest, I click on the map function on TripAdvisor (on the website, this is in the middle of the screen on the right) and group the landmarks by location in case I want to visit them on my own without a tour. If it costs too much to get transportation between the landmarks, or if I desire a deeper historical context from a guide, I consider booking a tour that includes as many of the landmarks on my list as possible.

Pay special attention to the reviews of the individual tours before choosing one. As always read the one-star reviews first to see if there are any major concerns and use common sense to filter out the complaining morons that plague apps such as TripAdvisor, Expedia, Yelp, and other online platforms. Also, be aware of the duration of the tour. Some tours will pick you up at your hotel, while others will require you to go to a meeting place.

Now that you are ready to book a tour, enter your destination on TripAdvisor and click on "Things to Do." Next, click on "Tours" on the website ("Tours & Sightseeing" on the app). Once you are ready to purchase a tour package, click on the "book" button. The link will take you to Viator, TripAdvisor's sister company that specializes in booking tours. From there, you can book in advance with a credit card. Viator will send you a confirmation email with a voucher for the tour. Some tour operators accept a voucher on your phone, while others will require a voucher to be printed out.

The confirmation email gives you a contact number for the tour company (usually on WhatsApp). You should contact your tour company a few days after booking and a few days before travel to confirm the tour and details such as start time, meeting place, or hotel pickup since occasionally discrepancies exist in the information listed in the tour description. If you do not confirm the tour a few days before travel, you run the risk of missing the opportunity to take the tour. This is more common when you are traveling off the beaten path due to internet connectivity issues or simply poor administrative skills on the part of the tour operator. After you take a tour, leave a review on TripAdvisor to help the tour company grow if you enjoyed the experience. If you had a lackluster or unpleasant experience, leave specific reasons in your review to inform travelers who follow your path.

Hop-on-hop-off bus tours

In chapter 3 (Using Layovers as a Tool), I mentioned hop-on-hop-off bus tours. These are not just a great option for a layover. I often take advantage of them in destinations in which I spend several days or more. Hop-on-hop-off bus tours take you to the most popular landmarks in a city. You can choose to stay at each attraction for a quick photo before you hop back on the bus, or spend some time exploring and take the next bus. They provide headphones for detailed pre-recorded information in eight different languages about each stop and even landmarks you may pass along the way.

It is a good idea to take this bus tour on the first or second day in a destination if possible because it gives you the lay of the land and puts a mental map in your head of the city, including landmarks or neighborhoods you may want to revisit to spend more time in. I have identified streets with restaurants and bars that look good to go eat, read a book, or simply take in the soul of a city. For links to a great international hop-on-hop-off-bus company, go to https://www.internationaltravelsecrets.com/travel-tools.

CHAPTER 6

HOTEL BOOKING SECRETS

I use Expedia for booking hotels, plain and simple. While you can use many of the other apps available for researching and booking hotels, Expedia's customer service is the most helpful and the website and app functionality are easy to navigate. Their customer service team has helped me negotiate refunds and gotten me out of some sticky situations while traveling abroad. They also allow you to accrue points that you can use for discounts on hotels. These discounts are not earth shattering, but a discount is a discount.

First, I set the filter to eliminate any hotels I would not choose to stay in. I do not need a five-star hotel, but in order to keep a minimum standard, be sure to check "air conditioning" and "free WiFi" in the filter as that will eliminate most of the less-desirable hotels right away. You can use many other filters to find a hotel to your personal liking. Other popular filters include price range, guest rating, property type (hotel, apartment, hostel, bed and breakfast, etc.), neighborhood, pet friendly, ocean view, and many more.

Hostels can run as low as $8 per night, but that is usually in a non-private room with bunk beds, which leaves your belongings vulnerable to thieves. Some hostels offer private room options for a higher price (usually ~$20 per night depending upon location). The room is very small, but if all you are doing is sleeping there, the size of the room does not matter. I have seen decent hotel rooms in the $25–$55 per night range in many locations. In some parts of the world (usually Western Europe), you will not be able to find non-hostel hotels for less than $90 per night. So sharing a room with your travel companion is a good way to keep this cost down.

I prefer to get a hotel that is close to the action or at least close to some cafes and restaurants so I can step out the front door and walk to a good spot without having to take a taxi every time. To do this, find a good location near any hotspots in the city using TripAdvisor, which is a website/mobile application not only for finding fun things to do but also booking tours, hotels, and flights. As you learned in the tour booking secrets chapter, TripAdvisor has a function in which you can indicate your destination and research attractions that interest you in that location. First, go to TripAdvisor and type in the name of the city. Click on "things to do." On the left side of the page is located a list of attractions by type. I usually click on the first option, which is "sights and landmarks," and then click "view map" on the right side of the page so I can see where the concentrations of these landmarks are located. I may even use this same procedure for restaurants to find any hotspots in a particular city.

Now that you have your TripAdvisor map on your screen, open up a new tab on your computer browser and go to the Expedia website. I first bring up a list of hotels in my price range on Expedia by using the appropriate filters mentioned above. On Expedia, click on "show map" on the left side of the page. At this point, you will have to go back and forth between the tabs and use your mouse to zoom in and line up the map of the landmarks on TripAdvisor as closely to the map of hotels on Expedia. Use this tactic to narrow down a neighborhood you would like to stay in and choose a hotel that fits your own personal standards and budget. For a free video on how to do this, go to https://www.internationaltravelsecrets.com/online-courses.

It is also a good idea to click on the published hotel photos on Expedia. You will get an idea of how your room and bathroom will be. Most of the time, you can see whether the rooms are decent or rat-infested just from the photos. In my experience, nine times out of ten, the photos can be trusted. In some instances, only photos from only the best rooms or recently remodeled rooms will be showcased. This happened to me in Algeria. When we got to our room, the bathroom was a plastic partition added to one corner of the room which did not even reach the ceiling, so there was little privacy and the smells easily migrated over the short walls. The showerhead released a single pee stream, which made it difficult to bathe. All we could do was laugh at the situation. So while most of the time the photos can be trusted, make sure to also check reviews.

It is important to screen the hotel reviews in order to make an informed decision. The first thing I do is view the one-star reviews to see if there are any trends across the feedback. Most one-star reviews are from morons who expect five-star conditions in third-world countries. Occasionally, however, I have found that many past guests have noted air conditioning that does not work or bug problems. You will notice a pattern across several reviews if there is a legitimate concern in a potential hotel. Use your best judgement when checking reviews for hotels you wish to stay in.

Once you have pegged a few hotels in a neighborhood you like, try using the street view on the Expedia map. As mentioned above, to get to the Expedia map, click on "View in Map" on the left of the Expedia page with the list of hotels in your chosen city. Once the map opens, you will see a yellow man in the upper right-hand corner. Click on the man and drag him to any street on the map, preferably near the hotels you are interested in. You may need to zoom in on the map first. This will give you an idea of how the neighborhood looks and whether the cafes and bars look inviting or dilapidated. I once found a hotel in Tbilisi that was centrally located. However, when I looked at the street view on the map, I noticed all the buildings around it were crumbling. Some walls on the surrounding buildings had even collapsed. The street seriously looked as if it had been bombed. Thus, we decided to choose a different hotel. Keep in mind that in locations off the beaten path, Google will not have as much on the ground coverage of locations, so you may only be able to find street views at busy intersections.

Why I don't use Airbnb

While Airbnb may be a good option in some areas, I try to avoid it whenever possible when traveling abroad. Airbnb is typically much cheaper than getting a hotel in the United States, but this is not always the case in other countries. Most of the time, I have found the prices to be as high as the cost of a hotel. Moreover, the service is not usually as good as it is in a hotel, and I prefer to have my toiletries restocked and towels replaced more often than an Airbnb host is typically willing to do.

In Serbia, we only received one toilet paper roll for the week to share between the three of us in the room. I had to contact the owner several times, and he brought an extra roll on the last day. Not the end of the world, but we had to resort to using restaurant bathrooms for most of the week.

Another issue occurred while traveling in Tajikistan. We informed the host that we would be arriving late at night and he acknowledged our request to be admitted at the scheduled time. We were left out in thirty-degree weather at an apartment building with fifty or so apartments, so we did not know where to go to inquire about our room—the owner only gave the street address of the building. A man outside offered to "sell" us information on where the owner was, but that was not the direction we wanted to go. Since the owner would not answer his phone after multiple attempts, we waited for three hours in the cold for a hotel in a different part of town to open.

Airbnb style rooms also appear on Expedia and other booking sites. The sites give you options for what type of accommodations you prefer such as "hotel" or "bed and breakfast." Avoid the choice listed as "apartment" as these are the Airbnb style accommodations. There are many Airbnb groupies out there, and if Airbnb is your speed, by all means, book away. I have had some positive experiences as well, but the negative experiences have outweighed the positive. I simply choose not to risk it when traveling abroad. Expedia is my friend.

CHAPTER 7

GROUND TRANSPORTATION SECRETS

One of the first things I research on a trip is the best way to get from the airport to the city center. It's as easy as searching Google for "best way to get from Madrid airport to the city center." You will find a combination of results ranging from buses to taxis to trains. While all options work, I prefer Uber, and luckily, the number of countries that offer Uber is growing every day. Uber always takes stored credit cards. Dealing with cash can be cumbersome as you have to consider the exchange rate and pay exorbitant ATM fees or currency exchange fees. The drivers are more trustworthy than traditional taxi drivers in many locations. I also can rest assured that the driver is taking a direct route, and I can follow said route on the Uber app right on my phone to make sure the driver is taking us where he is supposed to take us.

Taxis

Taxis are another popular option. While pricier than a bus or train, taking a taxi will get you to your destination faster without having to pay attention to the route as closely as you would while taking a train or bus. And if you're splitting the cost with your travel partner, it will be cheaper. If you opt for a taxi, it is imperative to research the typical fare for a trip to the city center, especially when interacting with opportunist taxi drivers who claim their meter is broken and charge an exorbitant rate to foreigners. Most of the time, I refuse to ride in a taxi with a "broken meter" as you will find the agreed-upon fare mysteriously increases once you get to the destination.

In some countries, the common practice is to have a flat rate from the airport to the city center. In this case, do not be afraid to hop in the taxi. I find it a good practice to have the driver write down the agreed-upon fare before getting into the car. This way it is more difficult for the driver to change the price once you arrive at your destination. Always handle all these things before you get in the car or begin loading your luggage. Once you get in the vehicle and the driver begins the trip, you have lost your leverage.

Do not be afraid to negotiate with taxi drivers as well. I often try this tactic after already having researched the typical fare. Sometimes I try it without knowing the typical fare. You will know you are not that far off from a fair amount if the taxi driver keeps following and pestering you. If a taxi driver leaves you alone after you take a hard line on an amount, you will know that your offer was too low. I always act as if I am not in a hurry and have gotten as much as a 50 percent discount on their original offer by waiting them out.

Early on in my travel adventures, I arrived at the airport in Vietnam and avoided the onslaught of taxi drivers fighting for my business by telling them I had some friends picking me up from the airport (use that excuse to give you time to assess the situation). I walked to the side and watched where the locals went to get a taxi, which was a bit further to the left of the exit doors. I found a ride to the city center for $10. My friends who arrived before me paid $100 for the same trip . . . and they speak the local language! Get the lay of the land before choosing your ride, and it can save you a lot of money. Be wary of taxi drivers who offer to take you to your destination in an unmarked car. Most likely the driver is simply trying to earn a living on the side, but drivers of these unmarked cars are more likely to participate in kidnapping or robbery schemes since they do not have a taxi company or government authority to answer to. This is not to say that taxi drivers who work for companies in marked cars do not participate in these schemes; they simply have more to lose if reported.

Many countries have a taxi desk inside the airport near the exit. You pay a predetermined fare at the desk and receive a coupon that you present to the driver at the front of the line of taxis outside the airport. This is a great way to avoid corruption and make tourists feel confident they are not being taken advantage of. A lot of these kiosks accept credit cards as well—added bonus!

Trains

Trains are a great option if you would like to save on transportation costs. Many get you from the airport to the city center for as little as $2 in some cases. I rarely see a train fare reach more than $12 or $15 to the city center. When this does happen, the area is just more expensive in general and a taxi or Uber can cost as high as $40 or $50 to get to the city center.

While they are cheaper, trains can be tricky to navigate, especially if you have to transfer to a different train at a particular station. I like to screenshot the map of the train stops on my phone in advance so I know if I am going in the right direction or not. This was a helpful tool one time when we jumped on the airport train in Amsterdam going in the wrong direction. Looking at the screenshot, I could tell that we were moving away from our intended stop and this saved us time. We were able to hop off as quickly as possible to wait for the train traveling in the opposite direction.

Buses

Buses are a cost-effective option, but I rarely use them. They often take more than twice the time to get from the airport to the city center and crime is common on buses in many locations. This is not to say I have never used a bus, but be sure to research the time and danger level at each location before deciding. Much like the train system, make sure you are familiar with the stops so you know which stop to take for your hotel or other intended destination. Remember to screenshot the map of the bus stops on your phone so you know if you are going in the right direction or not. This can save you valuable time, especially if you are checking out a city on a layover.

Airport pickup and drop off services offered by hotel

Always check to see if your hotel offers airport pickup and drop off services. This option can sometimes be reasonably priced, but more often than not, it can be a bit pricey if you are traveling with a friend or a small group since some hotels charge per person. Taxis and Uber can make for a cheaper ride since splitting the cost with your travel partner is an option. A strong upside to using the hotel for transportation, however, is that the driver is familiar with the location of the hotel. Sometimes taxi drivers or Uber drivers get lost adding to the time and cost of your fare.

CHAPTER 8

SAFETY TIPS & SECRETS

Safety while traveling is not just about avoiding getting robbed, it also entails knowing whether the food and water are safe, which vaccinations you need, and what world events may impact your journey. Follow the advice below to not just be prepared once you arrive but to also know about your chosen destination before you even book your ticket.

The throwaway wallet

To date, I have never been robbed while traveling. That said, I never carry all my credit cards and cash at once in case such a situation arises. I will usually carry one credit card at a time and a minimal amount of cash. And I carry a throwaway wallet at all times. I fill an old wallet with expired credit cards, library cards, old Jamba Juice cards—anything without too much personal information on it—in order to make the wallet look as real as possible. I also include leftover foreign currency from my previous travels. You will inevitably have leftover currency that does not have enough value to exchange. Use that leftover currency for this purpose. If you do face the unfortunate situation of getting robbed, handing the thieves a throwaway wallet can reduce the chance of being searched further, and by the time they notice the contents of the wallet are worthless, you will be well on your way to safety.

US Department of State website

The US Department of State website (travel.state.gov) publishes helpful information about each country in the world and serves as a valuable tool for travelers who venture abroad. In addition to entry and exit requirements, the website also lists currency restrictions, vaccination requirements, embassies and consulate locations, a description of the destination, special laws to be aware of, etc. One of the most important tools on the site is the safety rating. Each country is assigned a safety level ranging from 1 to 4 as outlined below:

1. Exercise normal caution

2. Exercise increased caution

3. Reconsider travel

4. Do not travel

Along with the ratings, they list specific warnings and news for regions in the country in question. Demonstrations at US embassies or recent terrorist attacks are commonly listed where applicable. One must take these warnings in stride, however. Occasionally a country will receive a higher danger rating if there are conflicts along a border with a neighboring country. Many times the city or region tourists visit are far from the areas labeled unsafe by the US Department of State. Level 4 countries include destinations such as Iran, Iraq, or North Korea. The US Department of State will all but tell you travel is not possible to countries that bear a level-4 rating.

Some reasons for a level 4 rating will be due to incidences of "terrorism, kidnapping, civil unrest, and armed conflict" and apply to countries such as Syria, Libya, Afghanistan, etc. North Korea is deemed a level-4 country because of a "serious risk of arrest and long-term detention of US nationals."[1] China has even been

1 "Country Information," Travel.State.Gov, U.S. Department of State, 2020, https://travel.state.gov/content/travel/en/international-travel/International-Travel-Country-Information-Pages.html.

listed as a level-4 country because of the outbreak of the coronavirus. The Department of State website warned in this situation: "The World Health Organization determined the rapidly spreading outbreak constitutes a Public Health Emergency of International Concern."[2]

While danger may be considerably higher in destinations such as Iraq where there are active bombings and military activity, many times a much different kind of caution is needed. You may remember the American who was sent to a North Korean labor camp for removing a propaganda poster from the hallway in his hotel. I have read a few travel blogs from those who venture into these so-called danger zones. Most state that if you use caution and mind your behavior to a special degree, these countries can offer a pleasant experience.

I remember joking with one of my travel partners about taking a "death trip," where we would visit North Korea, Iraq, and Iran. It was then that the idea hit me to research whether a large number of Americans had dared to visit such locations. The results were surprisingly inspiring. I learned of a sizable expat group in northern Iraq. Apparently, the Kurds in the region have a force of 100,000 troops and they are skilled at security measures that prevent groups such as ISIS from entering the area. I read that the Kurds are a warm and welcoming people and that visiting that region is becoming increasingly popular for American tourists with a stomach for adventure.

I also found some surprising results about visiting Iran. It turns out it is mostly the Iranian and US government that have issues with each other. I read about Iranians who spotted American tourists while at a demonstration in Tehran protesting US policy. A

2 "China International Travel Information," Travel.State.Gov, U.S. Department of State, December 2019, https://travel.state.gov/content/ travel/en/international-travel/International-Travel-Country-Information-Pages/China.html.

few of the protesters took the time to approach the Americans and explain that they have no ill-will toward the American people, but they simply dislike US foreign policy. The protesters welcomed the Americans and told them they were happy to have them visiting their country. Another story told of a lady who passed flowers to an American in a taxi cab apologizing for the traffic in her country. Again, special caution is advised despite the warm nature of the people. This is not a country I would advise getting inebriated and acting out or attracting attention to yourself in any way, but I would by no means avoid going based on this simple caveat. Recent tensions from the fallout of the strikes against Iranian general Soleimani in early 2020 have caused me to put off my plans of visiting Iran, but I plan to visit someday when the situation blows over.

Vaccinations

As mentioned previously, the Department of State offers information regarding entry and exit requirements of each country. This includes visa information, currency restrictions, and vaccination requirements. Most of the time vaccinations for those holding US passports are not required since many epidemics have been all but eradicated in the US. However, a few countries in Africa may still require yellow fever vaccinations and the like. At the time of this writing, obtaining a yellow fever vaccine can be problematic in the US as the only company that produces the vaccine transitioned to a new facility creating a production delay, resulting in a shortage over the past few years. This has caused the cost of the vaccine to reach as high as $400 per dose. One of the few companies that still has inventory is Passport Health. This company offers a variety of vaccinations based on the regions of the world in which you are traveling.

Do make your own choices with the recommendations,

though. I chose only to get vaccinations that are required for entry into a particular country. If I had chosen to go with all of their recommendations for the countries I was visiting, I would have walked out of the pharmacy with a $1,300 bill. My pharmacist, who also has experience traveling in Africa, stated that many of the recommended prescriptions and vaccinations are not necessary and that she fared just fine without them. I, too, took the plunge without most of the required vaccinations and made it out alive. Make your own choices based on your level of comfort or the size of your wallet.

To drink or not to drink

Many people, when traveling off the beaten path, fear drinking the local tap water. Many locations throughout the world have water that contains microorganisms that can cause minor, or on rare occasions, fatal illnesses for foreign travelers. The locals in the countries have developed an immunity to these impurities, so they have no problem drinking water from the tap. Keep in mind that, for the most part, all that travelers may suffer from when consuming tap water in these areas is diarrhea. It is, however, possible to contract hepatitis A, cholera, and typhoid fever from tap water in developing countries.

One thing many travelers forget is that ice cubes are also usually made from tap water, so use caution when ordering drinks in restaurants. It is also worth noting that it may be necessary for you to use bottled water when brushing your teeth, and to keep your mouth closed when showering. Although we do not necessarily drink large amounts of water when brushing our teeth or showering, we do inadvertently allow harmful microorganisms to enter our body when doing so in developing countries.

Like most of the warnings we have discussed in this text, some are overstated in many cases. According to many online resources, the only places that contain tap water that is safe to drink are North America, Western Europe, Australia, New Zealand, and only a few locations in Asia. I have had no problem brushing my teeth in most of Eastern Europe, in some countries in Asia, in South America, and in Africa. That is not to say that I never brush my teeth using bottled water. I definitely have on many occasions, but I refuse to believe that so few developed countries on Earth have safe tap water. Again, use discretion at your own comfort level here. All of our bodies react differently, and I do not want to ruin your trip by convincing you to be too bold in regards to drinking tap water in some regions of the world. Here is a complete list of countries that the CDC indicates are safe:

NORTH AMERICA
- Canada
- USA
- Greenland

EUROPE
- Iceland
- Ireland
- UK (England, Scotland, Wales, Northern Ireland)
- Western European countries west of and including Poland, Czechia, Austria, and Slovenia
- Greece

ASIA
- Hong Kong, Japan, Singapore, South Korea, Brunei, Israel (yes, Israel is in Asia)

OCEANIA
- Australia
- New Zealand

SOUTH AMERICA
- None

AFRICA
- None

Please note that some resources denote the tap water in Chile in South America and Saudi Arabia in Asia is safe to drink. For the most current list of water-safe countries, go to https://www.internationaltravelsecrets. com/travel-tools.

Is the food safe?

Sampling street food is a great (and tasty) way to experience local culture. Use good judgement when purchasing food from street vendors and sometimes even restaurants. It is better if the food is steaming when you receive it as you know it has not been sitting around growing harmful bacteria. If you can, look to see how clean the cooking areas, preparation spaces, and serving utensils are. Watch out for food that comes with its fair share of flies or other insects. Also, be on the lookout for the people in line for the street food. If locals are waiting for the street food at a food market, that is a good indicator that the food is not only good but also on the safer side. Sometimes there will be other tell-tale signs. On a trip to Ethiopia, we discovered a helpful hint: if there are more rats than people, move on to the next restaurant. Even with all of these precautions, you cannot guarantee that the food is safe. I ate all kinds of questionable food in Vietnam, and it wasn't the street vendors or questionable restaurants that got me . . . it was KFC that ended up giving me food poisoning.

CHAPTER 9

A FEW TIPS FOR FLYING

Flights can be the most painful part of your journey, especially those that surpass sixteen hours, such as the dreaded flight from LAX to Dubai or from LAX to Singapore. The secrets below will not only save you some money but will also allow you to arrive at your destination rested and prepared to conquer a new country.

Avoid the checked baggage fee by gate checking a bag

This works well with the tactic listed above. If you wait until the last minute to get on a plane, the overhead storage compartments may be full. This will allow you to check your bag at the gate. Most of the time you will be able to claim your bag at the arrival gate when you land instead of going to baggage claim. This is a good way to not have to deal with your larger carry-on bag during the flight, and the best part is that checking it at the gate is *free*! Always carry a backpack to hold the items you need to access during the flight such as phone chargers, headphones, and snacks!

Be the last person to board the plane

I will never understand why everyone is in such a hurry to get on the plane. Some people even pay extra to get on the plane first. If I am going to be stuck in a space smaller than a toilet seat for the next fourteen hours,

I will wait at the gate and stretch my legs as long as possible. Sometimes I even wait until the gate attendants call my name. Not only does this keep me out of that cramped seat for as long as possible but it also ensures I am not waiting in line on the jetway to get onto the plane. I cannot stand waiting on the jetway with my heavy carry-on bag, watching the people in front of me inching up before getting on the plane. I prefer to wait until the last minute and walk right on. If you are physically at the gate watching everyone board, you will not even come close to missing the flight. The flight attendants will always call the names of passengers who have checked in but have not boarded yet before closing the gate.

Some fight to get on board the plane as soon as possible to claim that ever-so-coveted overhead compartment space. I choose not to participate in that so-called luxury so I can relax while everyone else engages in the feeding frenzy. My carry-on is a large backpack that I place under the seat in front of me. My backpack holds everything I need to access while on a long flight so I do not need to bother my neighbor to get my headphones, snacks, or books from a bag in the overhead bin. I deal with the foot space by placing the bag on the floor against the front of my seat in order to stretch out my legs. I will then push the bag under the seat to bend my knees for a while and alternate between these two positions several times on a long flight. Since I am over six feet tall, I need to do more than this to remain comfortable for so many hours in a cramped space.

Comfort and killing time on flights

I routinely walk laps around the plane or do squatting exercises in some of the more open areas of the plane. This helps break up the time and prevents soreness from sitting in the same position for many hours at a time. You will feel much better by getting up and moving around during a long flight. Congregating in the galley or restroom areas is usually discouraged on shorter flights, but flight crews are much more forgiving on longer international flights. If you find a crew member bothering you about standing for too long in one of these areas, try going into the restroom to brush your teeth or splash some water on your face. You will usually be left alone if you are moving around and look like you are going back to your seat or to the bathroom area. This can give you much more standing time without being bothered by flight attendants.

A lot of fellow travelers ask me how I break up the time on a long flight. I am lucky that many of the international flights from LAX leave at 8 p.m. or later. This makes it easier to sleep at the normal time to kill a few of those monotonous flight hours. We all know that getting a good sleep on a plane is all but impossible. I consider it lucky to get four to five hours of sleep, even if it is not a deep sleep. The trade-off is that I will be tired enough to go to bed sooner, allowing my body to adjust to the new time zone as quickly as possible. I split the rest of the time on a flight between movies, TV shows, and books. Movies are a big winner for me as they kill at least two hours of flight time and I usually watch at least two—one before sleep and one after—if I can help it. Since the entertainment is free, I use the time to check out movies and TV shows that did not seem interesting enough to pay for back home, but these movies and shows become more intriguing when I have no other choice but to find something to pass the time.

Bring your own water onboard

Since sleeping while even slightly dehydrated can interfere with the quality of your sleep, staying properly hydrated allows you to arrive at your destination more rested and may also help prevent you from getting sick. Waiting for the beverage cart to offer you a few ounces of water a few times during the flight won't do the trick. And water bottles are very expensive to purchase on a flight (as much as $8 for a sixteen-ounce bottle). You can either purchase a liter of water for about $5 at an airport shop, or you can bring an empty bottle in your carry-on and fill it at an airport water dispenser after you have gone through security, of course. If you have a number of different flights on an international trip, this will save you a little extra money.

Bring your own food and snacks on board

Many don't know you can bring your own food and snacks on board an airplane. If you want to save the maximum possible amount of money, buy your food and snacks before entering the airport. Food items such as sandwiches, pizza, cooked meat, chips, nuts, chocolate, candy, pies, and cakes are allowed through security. Almost any food item that isn't composed mostly of liquid is allowed. However, spreadable items such as hummus, cheeses, butter, peanut butter, jam, etc. are limited by the 3.4-ounce rule. I sometimes buy food or snacks at the airport simply because cooked items will be a few hours fresher and I don't have to keep track of snacks until just before boarding. However, the price will be higher, so make your own choice based on the price-convenience factor.

Bring earplugs

Sleeping on planes is difficult enough due to the size and awkward angle of reclining airplane seats. The noise can also make it difficult. While you can't do anything about the seat itself, you can help the noise factor. Having a set of earplugs can drastically reduce the noise of people talking, babies crying, attendants announcing, etc. You will stay asleep longer and arrive slightly more rested. I like to keep a separate pair of earplugs in my toiletry kit so I don't have to remember to pack them. Always bring your toiletry kit in your carry-on bag so you have access to not only earplugs but also toothbrushes, toothpaste, aspirin, eye drops, sleeping pills, or any other items you may need for a longer flight.

Bring your own earphones

Earphones are one of the most important items to bring on long international flights. You will need them to listen to music, watch imperative time-passing movies and TV shows, or even to help you sleep. Some airlines charge for earphones, and some offer them at no charge, but one thing is for sure . . . the quality is poor. The airline standard-issue earphones usually do not fit right and the sound quality is right up there with the quality of the food offered on the plane. Bringing along your own earphones will save you a lot of money and give you a more quality experience.

Arriving three hours before your flight

Almost every airport recommends arriving three hours before an international flight. That's fine if you want to wait around for two and a half hours before you depart. All airports are different, but I routinely arrive at LAX (Los Angeles International Airport) an hour and a half or two hours before an international flight and I have never missed a flight from that airport. Typically, it takes five to fifteen minutes to drop off bags at LAX if I have checked in online prior to arriving. The lines to drop off bags are much longer the earlier you arrive since most people arrive so early before their flights. Therefore, by arriving a bit later in the cycle, you will not have to wait as long to drop off your bags. The security line typically runs fifteen to twenty-five minutes, in my experience. Use your personal preferences here. Some will trade a few extra hours of their time waiting in the airport in exchange for peace of mind. That's OK for people who spend $1,800 round trip. Since I rarely spend over $200 to fly out of the country, I'll spend those extra few hours at home, thank you.

CHAPTER 10

AIRLINE LOYALTY?

I often hear "You must have lots of airline miles saved up." Quite the opposite is the truth, actually. I do not subscribe to the concept of airline loyalty—especially for international travel. I choose an airline based on the best price. I do not worry much about service or meals or any of the other trivialities that can double or triple fares to a desired destination. I seem to find that generally, most airlines are the same. Most of the food is lackluster and the service is just enough to get you to where you need to go. Sure a few companies stand out beyond the rest, but not enough to justify the higher price, in my opinion. It doesn't hurt to sign up with a frequent traveler program with each airline as you will acquire points you can use to receive discounts even when you choose to fly an airline based on price. I am too lazy to do this since I do not want to take the effort to keep track of all the login information and points accrued, but for those of you who are more organized, this is not a bad idea. Engineers, don't get too excited: this is an excuse to create yet another spreadsheet. For a short list of airlines to embrace and airlines to avoid, go to https://www.internationaltravelsecrets.com/travel-tools.

Airlines to embrace and avoid

NORWEGIAN AIR— I choose Norwegian Air often because it is cheaper. This airline routinely offers flights from Los Angeles to Europe for under $200, but that is not the only reason I enjoy flying with them. Their planes are always brand new and are equipped with smart mood lighting or body-clock lighting. This blue lighting helps you sleep better. They also offer a steady flow of fresh air into the cabin so you can arrive at a destination more rested. The lower pressurized cabin and fresher, humidified air also contribute to the avoidance of jet lag. The windows are 65 percent larger and have an electronic feature that pixelates the window instead of having a physical window shade. This allows you to electronically dim the amount of light coming through the window or block it out completely. Additionally, the seats are equipped with personal screens, so you can order drinks, food, blankets, and such from your seat. No more pushing the attendant call button and waiting for them to come take your order. You can also leave your tab open so that all your orders get charged to your card at the end of the flight.

EMIRATES—Emirates is the largest airline in the Middle East. The airline boasts it has the most modern fleet of Boeing 777 and A380 in the world. Believe it or not, the planes actually have showers and lounge bars. Emirates has some of the best service and best food of most of the airlines I have flown. It is rare for me to request seconds when consuming airline food, but Emirates has what I would consider to be restaurant-quality food, and all the dishes are halal.

QATAR AIRWAYS—On a flight from the Philippines to Qatar, my travel companion was feeling extremely sick and was in tears from the havoc the air pressure was having on her sinuses. She found out later she had bronchitis, which we all know is difficult to take while on the ground not to mention in the air on a long flight. The flight attendant went above and beyond by dipping into the airplane medical supplies to offer her medicine to alleviate her symptoms. He also checked up on her frequently and brought extra water often throughout the flight. It did not cure her of her ills, but it did lessen her suffering enough to get to the next destination. I will always remember the display of customer service, and while I typically choose flights based on price, I do enjoy seeing Qatar Airways on my itinerary whenever it pops up.

MALAYSIA AIRLINES—On a flight from Singapore to Brunei, a flight attendant sang and played several songs on his ukulele including "I'm Yours" by Jason Mraz as we boarded the plane. He played so well that I still have the video saved on my phone to this day. I had the pleasure of sitting near the flight attendant during takeoff and landing and found that he was of Malaysian descent but was born in the US. He shared that he had been working in the corporate world and quit his job to work for the airline because he wanted to travel the world. We swapped travel stories and the time on the flight passed quickly. Sure they may lose a plane or two every now and then, but this Malaysian Airlines flight was one of the more memorable ones due to a little extra musical touch. Not sure if live musical entertainment is standard operating procedure, but good call.

KOREAN AIR—Some of you will boycott this airline and some of you will book a ticket right away. Korean Air has a unique set of guidelines for its airline stewardesses. The company usually will not hire stewardesses over twenty-seven and focuses on those that would be considered most attractive to guests. In addition, all stewardess applicants must have a college degree. The airline is strict about how the stewardesses maintain their weight and tend to favor those with straight teeth and clean complexions. Rules such as these wouldn't fly in the US (no pun intended), but each country has its own standards and preferences.

AIR BALTIC—By far the worst airline I have ever flown is Air Baltic. In my experience, they have zero customer service and even seem to bask in the opportunity to complicate your trip. I am not a demanding person and can deal with poor customer service. This airline, however, goes above and beyond to ensure that you do not have a pleasant experience. I have had two very bad experiences:

We were flying from Norway to Czechia with a layover in Lithuania. We had checked our bags all the way through to the final destination and paid the baggage fee for both travelers in advance. They tried to charge my friend a second time for a baggage fee when we were boarding the plane from our layover in Riga. I showed them evidence that we had already paid for our luggage in advance. This carried no weight with the airline counter agent. After much discussion, I finally refused to pay the fee since I had already paid it and had proof, so the agent called a supervisor from upstairs to address the situation. She pretended to not know what a layover or a transfer was and she works for an airline . . . nice try! She also told me that because I was causing a problem that she was now going to also charge me for my baggage fee a second time as well—all with a smug smile. She told us that we could either pay the baggage fees again or stay in Riga. This is where I lost it. I decided to not interrupt our trip and told her, "I WILL get my money back" and promised her that she would NOT win. She knew I was serious because she wrote down our details while I was paying so that she could inform the powers that be to not issue me a refund. Little did she know, I was not even going to waste my time with the airline. So far as I can tell with Air Baltic is that the higher the position, the higher the smugness and unwillingness to help. When I returned home, I called my credit card company and simply disputed the charge. The credit card company immediately reversed the charge. Michael: 1. Air Baltic: 0.

When I flew from Portland to Lithuania, the person

I flew with on this trip happens to have two last names. We booked his flight with his full legal name. However, his passport only bears one of the last names since both of them did not fit on his passport application. I am aware of the rule that requires a passenger to book the tickets in the name that appears on the passport of the traveler, but all of the other twelve airlines we flew on this particular around-the-world trip accepted the name discrepancy when my friend produced his driver's license along with his passport since the license bore his full name and proved that he was the same person. Air Baltic was the only airline that did not oblige him and required him to purchase a new last-minute ticket at a severely elevated price. All of the representatives from Air Baltic were smiling with pleasure at the fact that my friend had to purchase a new ticket even though he had already purchased a ticket for the same exact flight. Even when we went up to the airline offices to see if we could get an exception similar to the one offered by all the other airlines, the supervisor was even more disagreeable than the representatives who worked under her. I told my friend about my previous experience and how to dispute the charge. He also got a refund. Suck it, Air Baltic!

CHAPTER 11

PACKING & LUGGAGE SECRETS

Packing seems like a relatively easy task for many, but I have included some tips that will assist you in taking less on the road. And by following the tips, you can also add convenience and ease to your future travels.

Pack a trash bag, grocery bag, and dryer sheets in your luggage

I always bring a trash bag to stash my dirty clothes, keeping them separate from the clean clothes. I even add a few dryer sheets to the mix to keep up that fresh smell as clothes can get a bit musty or even smelly (even if separated) if you have been doing a lot of hiking in hot weather. Also, pack a grocery bag for your bathing suit if it does not have enough time to dry before you have to get on the next plane. There is nothing worse than your wet bathing suit making the rest of your clothes wet, creating a mildew smell on all your clean clothes.

Pack one outfit in your carry-on

I always pack at least one outfit in my carry-on in case the airline loses my checked luggage. It is a good idea to include your toiletry bag and any chargers or universal plugs for that same reason. This is especially needed if you have short layovers in Europe. It is common to have thirty to forty-five-minute layovers in Europe, which makes it difficult for the airport ground crew to unload the baggage, transport it to another section of the airport, and have it loaded onto another plane before the next flight leaves the gate for the runway. Plan on not having your bag when you see extremely short layovers. If I come across one of these while planning a trip, I make sure to at least be in the next location for at least two days to give a potentially lost bag enough time to catch up to me.

Limit the number of shoes you bring

I used to bring sandals, walking shoes, and dress shoes on all my trips. Others bring those I listed in addition to matching shoes for different outfits. I now purchase walking shoes that are black and stylish so they can pass as shoes for a nicer outfit if necessary. It's not ultra-glamorous I'll admit, but it gets the job done and keeps my bag lighter while offering a little extra room for packing. Bring a nicer pair of walking shoes and a pair of sandals and you've got all you need to deal with just about any situation while traveling. For a complete packing list go to https://www.internationaltravelsecrets. com/travel-tools.

Make your luggage stand out

Most luggage is black, gray, or silver making it hard to tell whose is whose at baggage claim. If you aren't brave enough to buy chartreuse luggage with Teletubby images all over it, you can easily make your bag stand out with one of these simple tricks I have observed at the airport:

1. Tie a ribbon or scarf around the handle
2. Place a sticker or stickers on the large surface of the bag (for hard cases only)
3. Use duct tape to make a design on the side such as an X or the first letter in your name

4. Write your last name neatly on it using a marker or paint

We all have seen variations of this at the airport. My current luggage is black with thin neon green trim around the edges, so it is easy to spot. However, when the mileage on that bag has caused a wheel to break or a zipper to split, I will employ one of these ideas. Yup, I think I gotta go with the Teletubbies.

Traveling with only a carry-on

Even with all the air hours I have logged, I have not yet graduated to this line of thought. However, I do not believe it is a bad idea, and I may switch to this method soon. As I mentioned elsewhere in this text, I usually travel with a medium-sized piece of luggage that I check and a large backpack that I use as my carry-on. Other seasoned travelers maintain that they use laundromats or hotel laundry services when they travel, which allows them to bring less clothing to avoid checking a bag. That is the dilemma. Checking bags is rarely free and can cost as much as $99 to check per flight. Most of the time the cost is between $30 and $60—if you book in advance. I once missed a flight on my way home from Paris and had to pay $99 to check the bag since we booked a replacement flight last minute.

Some swear by the carry-on only to avoid these fees. However, I usually pay the baggage fee since my stops are usually too short to allow the hotel enough time to get the clothes back to us if we were to have them washed. I also do not want to be tied to a laundromat for an hour or two while waiting for my clothes to finish being washed and dried. I have, however, heard from other travelers I meet that it is possible to bring only a few outfits and wash them in the sink or bathtub with some detergent or other form of soap. They will hang dry their clothes after wringing them out or, as I heard on my last trip, roll their wet clothes up tightly in a towel to bring out excess water before hanging them up. I am considering this option as it shortens the time of having to wait in line to check and reclaim a bag and can save hundreds of dollars each trip depending upon how many flights I take. It seems like a lot of extra work, but I'll give it a shot on a shorter trip and see how I like it.

CHAPTER 12

VISAS AND PASSPORTS

Some countries require you to apply for a visa in order to enter their borders. A visa grants you permission to stay in a country for a set period of time, usually ranging from several days to several months. Since visa formalities vary greatly depending upon your chosen destination, I recommend doing a little research before planning your next trip. A great tool for checking visa requirements for your desired destination is the US Department of State website (https://travel. state.gov/content/travel/en/international-travel/ International-Travel-Country-Information-Pages.html). Most of the information on the site is up to date, but I sometimes verify visa requirements on the actual country's consulate website. The Department of State website also requires you to check visa requirements for each country one at a time, which can be time consuming if you are visiting multiple countries on one trip. For a comprehensive list of visa requirements by country all on one page, go to https://www. internationaltravelsecrets.com/travel-tools (this is for US citizens only).

I do not want to get stuck at the airport for lack of a visa after prepaying for hotels and tours. Thus, it is important to research this before even booking your flight as some countries' visa application processes can take up to thirty days to complete. Most European countries allow for a visa on arrival (VOA) in which the stamp in your passport or, in some cases, even simply filling out an arrival card will suffice for obtaining entry. Costs for a VOA range from FREE to $100 or more. Countries such as Luxembourg do not even have customs. That's right! You can walk right off the plane and into the city without having to show your passport.

Other countries require you to apply in advance for a visa, which cuts out the paperwork after landing completely. Some visa processes simply require you to enter your passport information, while others may require you to submit passport-size photos, copies of your passport, airline itinerary, and hotel information. As time goes on, many countries are offering this service online, which is convenient since you can upload necessary documents or photos and pay using a credit card all on the consulate website. Most countries that offer online services grant visas the same day. Others grant visas within a few days and send the visa via email.

Countries such as Russia or Algeria have a much more complicated visa application process, which includes obtaining a visa in the weeks (or months) before you even depart for your trip. These countries require you to mail your actual passport to the consulate along with a money order and a complicated application packet. They may ask for bank statements to prove you have the means to leave the country and do not become a financial burden. They may also require you to list all of the countries you have visited over the past ten years in order including all of the dates. Russia even requires an invitation letter which most hotels will offer once you book with them. This means you will have to book a hotel before you apply for a visa, so be sure to book a hotel that is refundable in case your visa application is not approved.

The visa application process can be painstaking and allows for many mistakes. Keep in mind most countries will keep your visa fee even if your application gets rejected for a simple mindless mistake. For instance, Algeria may reject your application if you do not fill it out in all capital letters. If you are great with details and follow the directions line by line, complete the process yourself. If you are not detail-oriented, you can use a variety of available services that check any application paperwork for errors prior to submission for a nominal fee. Some even prepare the application for you and submit on your behalf.

Israel and entry limitations to Muslim countries

It is worth noting that if you visit Israel, some Muslim countries will deny you entry. Since several Muslim countries do not acknowledge Israel as a sovereign nation, they punish those who have visited Israel by not granting them entry. The good news is that Israel no longer stamps passports. Visitors who arrive at international airports in Israel receive a small blue arrival card or "stay permit" in lieu of a passport stamp. You must carry this card with you at all times. It may be requested to rent a car or to enter and return from certain areas of the West Bank or Gaza Strip.

No stamp in your passport means that there will be no evidence of your visit to Israel should you try to enter any of the Muslim countries that do not acknowledge Israel as a sovereign nation. However, you should consider a few details: If you departed Israel through a land border into neighboring Jordan or Egypt, you will not have an Israeli exit stamp, but you will have an entry stamp from a location that officials know borders Israel, and you may get denied access. If you already have such a stamp in your passport, do not be afraid to order a new passport if you would like to sidestep this issue completely. Also, check your luggage for any airline barcode stickers that indicate that you flew into an international airport in Israel as those can also result in denied entrance into some Muslim countries. Please note that you will be asked either in person, on arrival cards, or on visa applications whether you have been to Israel. How you answer the question is up to you. Below is a list of Muslim countries that allow visitors who have traveled to Israel, and those countries that do not. Please keep in mind that information is constantly changing based on world affairs and tensions between nations, so please be sure to verify any information in this book before making concrete travel plans.

Muslim countries that allow visitors who have traveled to Israel:

- Algeria, Bahrain, Bangladesh, Egypt, Indonesia, Kurdistan (in northern Iraq), Jordan, Malaysia, Morocco, Oman, Qatar, United Arab Emirates, Tunisia, Turkey.

Muslim countries that do not allow visitors who have traveled to Israel:

- Afghanistan, Iran, Iraq, Kuwait, Lebanon, Libya, Pakistan, Saudi Arabia, Sudan, Syria, Yemen

Some of the countries in the above list are not as adamant about the restriction as Lebanon or Iraq. Iran, for example, allows you entry as long as your visit to Israel took place more than 6 months before your arrival in Tehran. Saudi Arabia has also loosened its restriction recently.

Additional questioning when exiting Israel

Be sure to allow extra time when departing Israel by plane. Security agents question all passengers and x-ray your luggage before you even get to the check-in desk. While I have read that this questioning process can take up to an hour, mine was complete in about fifteen minutes. Do not be alarmed at the questions as the security agents are firm but professional. The more you have traveled, the more you will be questioned — especially if you have visited any Arab countries. Some of the questions are basic such as where you live or what your profession is. They sometimes ask deeper questions such as how I met the person I am traveling with and when. They even asked me how many countries he had been to. I had no idea of the exact number, and the agent seemed dismayed that I didn't know the answer. There is nothing unusually alarming about the process. Just know that it will take some additional time before checking in.

Get an expanded passport

Normal passports come with twenty-four pages. However, you have the option to get an expanded passport with fifty-two total pages at no additional cost. I recommend this option if you plan on traveling a lot since it does not cost any additional fees for the expanded version. It used to be possible to have extra pages added later by mailing your passport off to have them inserted. It made the passport a bit clumsy, but it did the job. However, nowadays you have to get a completely new passport if your current passport is full. The process is similar to the renewal process and it does come with additional fees. This is a welcomed change since the old method of simply adding pages to an existing passport made it more likely that you would experience problems from customs agents in foreign countries with strict entry policies. I once was questioned in Belarus about the additional pages that were added to my passport. I believe the agent had never seen an addition and thought that either the passport was fake or that I added them myself. He brought over his supervisor to examine the passport, and after I answered several accusatory questions, they let me pass.

Passport with added pages

Six-month passport rule

Passports expire every ten years. However, do not plan a trip if you are getting close to six months left before your passport expires. You will not be allowed to board the plane in most cases because many countries do not want you stuck within their borders with an expired passport unable to get home. Some countries have a three-month rule or even less. However, it is a good idea to renew your passport well before the six-month point, just in case. You can renew your passport at any time, and if you renew it nine months before the expiration date, you can avoid this issue altogether.

Make copies of your passport

Always make copies of your passport. Put one in your backpack and one in your larger bag, whether it be a checked bag or your other carry-on. You will need these copies if you lose your passport. Also, scan your passport and email it to yourself before you leave. That way you will have access to it even if you lose your other copies. Remember that your passport is the most important item that you bring on your trip. You cannot leave home without it, and it is more than difficult to return without it. Thus, it should be first on all your packing lists. What a disappointing predicament it would be to arrive at the airport excited to leave on your trip only to find that you left your passport on your dresser. Most of us live too far from the closest international airport to have enough time to retrieve a left-behind passport without missing our scheduled flight. You can burn all the rest of your belongings in your bag as long as you have this important document. Read the story about how I lost my passport in Tanzania in the unforgettable moments section below for a personal experience I had with this.

CHAPTER 13

FOREIGN CURRENCY SECRETS

As technology improves around the world, the need for carrying cash continues to diminish. Uber worldwide has reduced the need for cash for taxis in much of the world. Even taxis and train depots accept credit cards in many locations nowadays. I usually only carry cash for street food vendors or to purchase artisan crafts from local shops. Most everything else can be purchased on a credit card. However, some countries have not caught up yet. For instance, Iran is a cash-only society. Because of the economic sanctions, western credit cards do not work since most banks are not allowed to do business in the country. Other countries such as Algeria simply have not caught up yet since tourism has not yet discovered this beautiful destination.

That said, I try to avoid using cash as much as possible. Cash can be stolen or lost, and it does not offer the benefits of using a credit card for travel expenses. Through using a credit card, I can track what I spend, earn points for my purchases, and avoid foreign exchange fees which can take a large bite out of your currency when you exchange cash. Foreign exchange fees are what currency changers charge for their service of changing your US dollars into the local currency. It can sometimes cost as much as 20 percent. This can be alleviated by bringing cash with you on your trip.

Clean crisp $100 bills usually get the best exchange rate. Avoid using money changer booths at the airport whenever possible as those will be the most expensive. Hotels and shops often offer the better rates if you have to use this route. Do not be afraid to ask for the exchange rates at a few places in the neighborhood in which you are staying.

ATMs are a good option for getting cash only when you need to instead of lugging a large amount of cash from home that can be lost or stolen before you get a chance to use it. However, keep in mind you will be paying three fees when you use ATMs: an ATM fee from the ATM you are using in the country you are visiting (usually $5), a non-branch ATM fee from your bank in the US (also usually $5), and foreign transaction fees which run between 2 and 3 percent of the total transaction. Having a combined flat $10 ATM fee for withdrawals, it is good to withdraw enough the first time so you do not have to keep going back for more cash and get charged multiple times as a result. On the flip side, if you pull out too much, you will have to exchange the cash back into US dollars for an additional fee, so use good judgement when withdrawing cash. Also, beware of strangers offering to change cash for you as they are often scams to distribute counterfeit currency. You also do not want a stranger knowing where you keep your cash or how much you have. Taxi drivers and people stalking the arrivals section of the airport often look for unsuspecting tourists to utilize their "exchange services." Many will offer you drugs as well, so that should tell you what you are dealing with.

Avoid ATM fees

You can avoid the ATM fees by opening a bank account at a bank that is part of the Global ATM Alliance. The Global ATM Alliance allows customers of several banks across the globe to avoid ATM fees by using partner branches. If you have a Bank of America account, you are already part of this alliance. If you choose not to open a Bank of America account, you can open an account at any one of the banks in the alliance and enjoy fee-free withdrawals in most cases. Other banks that are part of the Global ATM Alliance are Barclays, BNP Paribas, Banca Nazionale del Lavoro, Deutsche Bank, Scotiabank, and Westpac. Be aware that banks on this list come and go due to mergers and other transactions. Also, some banks on this list have ATMs that are not considered part of the alliance depending upon which country the ATM is located in.

If you do not want to be tied to this list of banks, you can open a Schwab Bank High Yield Investor Checking Account. When you use the Schwab checking account debit card, the bank will reimburse any "eligible" ATM fees charged by other institutions. Schwab does not define what eligible ATM fees are, but according to the website, "unlimited ATM fee rebates apply to cash withdrawals using the Schwab Bank Visa® Platinum Debit Card wherever it is accepted. ATM fee rebates do not apply to any fees other than fees assessed for using an ATM to withdraw cash from your Schwab Bank account. Schwab Bank makes its best effort to identify those ATM fees eligible for rebate, based on the information it receives from Visa and ATM operators." Unlike other banks that offer this perk, Schwab also does not have a minimum balance requirement in order for it to kick in.

There are other traditional banks, credit unions, and online banks that offer reimbursements for ATM fees. However, many of them limit the reimbursement to $10 or $20 in fees per statement cycle. Some even require you to maintain a minimum balance in order to get access to this perk. Check with your current bank to see what perks they offer in relation to international ATM withdrawals. If it does not fit your needs, open an account at one of the institutions mentioned above.

Currency conversion

One of the challenges of traveling to several countries in one trip is getting accustomed to the currency conversion in your head. A great tool is the currency converter on Google. Type the currency of the country you are visiting into the search bar on your browser; for example, Thailand Baht to USD, and a converter calculator will automatically load on your phone or computer. I like to research this before I leave and know how much of a country's currency equals $10 or $20, so I know how much I am being charged for transportation, food, or souvenirs.

Use caution as some restaurants around the world will offer you prices in dollars and some will offer you prices in the local currency. Usually, the purpose is to make things easier for the tourist. However, sometimes a shopkeeper or bartender will go back and forth between the local currency and dollars to get you to spend more. This happened to me at a bar in Tel Aviv. When we were keeping track of what we spent on food, cigars, and drinks, the bartender switched back and forth between shekels and dollars. She quoted us 550 for the final bill, which we thought was in shekels. Much to our chagrin, the bill was in dollars meaning we spent $550 for two people that night. Oh well. I do not remember much of that night anyway since some British and Canadian travelers kept buying us shots. I was hoping my credit card statement would forget to include the charge. No such luck.

CHAPTER 14

USING YOUR CELL PHONE ABROAD

Avoid international calling rates by using WiFi, WhatsApp, FaceTime

Calling home or accepting calls while traveling can cost anywhere from $0.25 to $2 per minute. You can avoid expensive phone usage costs by using internet calling through certain apps while connected to WiFi. FaceTime, Facebook Messenger, Snapchat, and WhatsApp are the most common, but there are a few more that vary in popularity by region. If you meet a traveler from China, you will most likely only be contacting them on WeChat, for instance. While WhatsApp tends to be the most prevalent across the globe, be prepared to download several different apps if you plan to stay in communication with new friends while traveling the world.

Use phone maps without an international data roaming plan

Many people are not aware that their map apps work using a satellite, not data or WiFi. Sure using data or WiFi drastically improves the functionality of your map app, but it is not 100 percent necessary. One issue of only using a map app with a satellite is that the map takes a long time to load, and when it does, it will only load in the immediate area. Zooming out too far causes the larger area of the map not to load. Thus, I always opt to get an international data roaming plan because I do not want to risk getting stuck somewhere without the full use of my map. However, if you are traveling on a shoestring budget, this is a good option to save potentially $100 or more.

Cell phone international data roaming plans

If you are going to travel abroad, you will need to use data on your phone. You will need it to use your map app, operate email to find airline and tour reservations, use TripAdvisor for finding landmarks and restaurants, and contact Uber for transportation to name a few. Unfortunately, it can be expensive to add this service to your phone. Depending upon your carrier, plans can range from FREE to $140 for thirty days. It is true that you can sometimes avoid using data while using WiFi at your hotel or at certain cafes, but not all destinations have reliable WiFi, so it is not a good idea to solely rely on that. Below I have compared some of the larger carriers:

SPRINT—Sprint offers international data roaming and texting for free. International calls are only $0.25 per minute. However, the downside to Sprint is that even while at home, you cannot receive texts, search the internet, or use any apps that require data while you are on phone calls (unless you are connected to the internet). This isn't a problem while at home, but if you need to look something up while on the phone at a mall or in a car away from WiFi, it can be quite limiting. I switched to Sprint for the free international data roaming, but there was definitely a sacrifice to make for the savings.

VERIZON—Verizon offers what is called TravelPass. It costs $10 per day for every day you use it, and you can access your domestic voice, text, and data plan while traveling in over 185 countries worldwide. You will only be charged on the days you use your phone outside the US. This is a great option if you are gone for seven days or less. If you're traveling longer, Verizon offers cost-effective monthly international plans. For $70 a month, you get 0.5 GB of data, 100 minutes of talk, and 100 sent text messages (text messages received are free). For a $130 a month, you get 2 GB of data, 250 minutes of talk, and 1000 sent text messages (text messages received are free). If you go over any of the limits for the included services, the cost will be $25 for every 0.5 GB of data, $0.35 per minute of talk, and $0.05 for every sent text message. The monthly international plans are one-time charges or you can set it up as recurring if you travel enough to necessitate that.

AT&T—AT&T offers what is called International Day Pass. It costs $10 per day for every day you use it, and you can access your domestic voice, text, and data plan while traveling. You will only be charged on the days you use your phone outside the US. This is a great option if you are gone for seven days or less. If you're traveling longer, AT&T offers monthly international plans that are more cost-effective. For $70 a month, you get 2 GB of data, $0.35 per minute of talk, and unlimited text messages. For $140 a month, you get 6 GB of data, $0.35 per minute of talk, and unlimited text messages. If you go over any of the limits for the included services, the cost will be $30 for every GB of data, $0.35 per minute of talk, and $0.05 for every sent text message. The monthly international plans are one-time charges, or you can set it up as recurring if you travel enough to necessitate that.

T-MOBILE—T-Mobile offers what is called International One-Day Pass. It costs $5 per day for every day you use it, and you can access 512 MB of data and unlimited calling while traveling. You will only be charged on the days you use your phone outside the US. You can also get the 5 GB International Pass. For $35, you get 5 GB and unlimited calling for up to ten days. The 15 GB International Pass is $50 and includes 15 GB along with unlimited calling for up to thirty days. T-Mobile offers monthly international plans that can be more cost-effective than the options listed above. The T-Mobile Magenta Plan is a domestic plan that for $70 per month already includes unlimited international texting, unlimited data, and Gogo in-flight privileges (1 hour of in-flight WiFi and unlimited texting). The next step up is the Magenta Plus Plan. It costs $85 per month, which includes unlimited international texting, unlimited data, and Gogo in-flight privileges (unlimited in-flight WiFi and unlimited texting). All calls from the Magenta plans are 25 cents per minute.

Universal outlet adapters and portable cell phone chargers

A handy tool to pick up is a universal outlet adapter. Size and shape of outlets in different continents vary, so your North American plugs may not fit unless you are staying in one of those rare hotels that has universal outlet strips in each room. Also, the voltage is different in many regions across the globe, which can fry whatever electronics you try to plug in. Thus, you will want an adapter. Universal outlet adapters allow you to plug your North American device into the adapter, while the adapter fits to whichever outlet shape and voltage is in the wall at your hotel.

It is also important to bring an external charger while out and about on long tours many hours away from your hotel. Taking pictures and videos while using GPS can quickly gobble up that coveted battery life. There is nothing worse than missing that perfect photo or not being able to find your way back to your hotel because your phone battery died. Be sure to purchase an external charger that can charge your phone more than once before needing a recharge itself. I have one that offers up to three full charges and it is not that much more expensive. **Make sure to pack both your universal outlet adapter and your external charger in your carry-on bag in case the airline loses your checked baggage.** That way you won't be stuck without power while waiting for the airline to deliver your bag. For a list of the best universal adapters, chargers, and other travel tools I use, go to https://www. internationaltravelsecrets.com/travel-tools.

Charging your phone in an airport

Often you will find those coveted outlets at airport charging stations are full. Sometimes outlets are sparse at airports in third-world countries. Not to worry as all you need to do is plug in your charger to a USB port on the back of any television set whether it be a TV showing the news or a flight status monitor. Most of the time airport personnel will leave you alone, but be discreet in order to avoid the attention of an overly dutiful employee out to save the world.

CHAPTER 15

SCAM: CREDIT CARDS WITH TRAVEL REWARDS

Absolutely, never, ever, EVER, sign up for a credit card that boasts travel rewards in the form of accruing travel points. It is a complete scam. While you may get free flights or hotels, the point to price ratio is skewed and you are overpaying for these perks. Why do you think they employ a complex point conversion system instead of simply having each point accrued equal to a dollar? The reason is the credit card companies do not want consumers to figure out how little in rewards they actually receive per dollar spent. If consumers knew how little they actually got from all the spending they do, they would most likely cancel all of their travel rewards cards. A long time ago I used credit card points for a flight that used up the equivalent of $750 on a flight that I found on my own for less than $300. Even worse, many airline miles earned on a credit card expire, making your efforts wasted if you do not use them in the allotted time frame.

That said, you are better served getting cards that credit your account balance with cash. This way you can get a check or account credit at the end of the year to use toward your travel (or whatever else you choose). Some even allow you to cash in your rewards at any time of the year for an account credit with the simple push of a button—and cash rewards never expire. If, however, you are the type of person who is not disciplined enough to set aside the cash you earn from credit card rewards, using a travel rewards card may be a good option for you. You will reap a lot less in reward value per dollar spent, but at least you will get your free or discounted flights and get yourself traveling.

There are many credit card rewards options out there, but my favorites are Synchrony Bank cards offered through Costco and Sam's Club, and Capital One *Quicksilver*. My Synchrony Bank card offers 5 percent back on gas, 3 percent back on travel and dining out, and 1 percent on everything else. **This credit card does not charge foreign transaction fees which is great for making purchases while traveling abroad.** Foreign transaction fees usually run between 2 percent or 3 percent of every transaction and can add up fast. I use the Synchrony Bank card for all my gas, travel, and dining expenses. At the end of the year, I deposit the check I receive into my account or credit it toward my statement balance.

The Capital One *Quicksilver* card offers 1.5 percent back on *all* purchases. I can redeem the cash for an account credit directly from the Capital One app. **This credit card also does not charge foreign transaction fees**. Last year I received over $5,000 combined in cash that I used to fund my travel expenses. Avoid the credit card travel point scam and use the cash back as a means to fund your travel. For a complete list of the best credit cards to use, go to https://www.internationaltravelsecrets. com/travel-tools. This comprehensive list will show you which cards have the highest rewards, lowest annual fee, and free foreign transactions.

One way to increase the number of rewards you receive is to put all your bills and other expenses on your credit cards. Medical insurance, utility, cell phone, car insurance, charities, home insurance, and cable/ streaming service companies usually give you an option to pay automatically with a credit card. I charge all my food, gas, and travel on my credit cards as well. This is how I maximize my rewards to use toward free travel. Do not use this option if you are not disciplined enough to pay off the credit card balance each month. If you do not pay off the statement balance each month, you will be charged high interest (usually upwards of 25 percent).

Credit cards with VIP airport lounge access

Another perk to consider when perusing credit card choices is VIP lounge access at airports. Lounges are a great way to relax away from the crowds. While the quality of services will vary greatly by city and country, many lounges offer free WiFi, free food, and free drinks including alcohol. Free bottled water and fruit juices can be refreshing while waiting for your next flight to board. Some lounges offer beer and wine, while others will have several forms of liquor. Food offerings range from light snacks to full buffet-style meals, depending upon location. I've had excellent food at airport lounges, but I have also had to wander out into the regular airport to buy food at a restaurant when the free food doesn't quite suit my taste.

At a VIP lounge in Beijing, I was even able to take a shower for free before boarding the plane. This was convenient for me because we had booked a layover tour in which the tour guide picked us up at the airport and drove us to the Great Wall of China. The lift that transported people to the wall was broken, so we had to unexpectedly climb thousands of steep stairs in extremely hot and humid weather. Had I gotten on the plane without a shower, my neighbor would have been most certainly displeased.

Priority pass for airport lounges

If access to airport lounges is not available as a perk for one of your existing credit cards, it is possible to purchase a Priority Pass Membership. This option is only for those who really want to experience lounge life because the annual memberships can be pricey. As of this writing, the three membership tiers are $99, $299, and $429 annually. Depending upon your membership level, extra fees may apply:

STANDARD $99

- Plus $32 fee for each lounge visit
- Plus $32 fee for each friend you bring

STANDARD PLUS $299

- 10 free visits
- Plus $32 fee for each additional lounge visit
- Plus $32 fee for each friend you bring

PRESTIGE $429

- Free member visits
- Plus $32 fee for each friend you bring

Please visit https://www.prioritypass.com/en/members-benefits for up-to-date membership benefits.

CHAPTER 16

SCAM: TRIP CANCELLATION INSURANCE

To buy trip cancellation insurance or to not buy trip cancellation insurance . . . I have never purchased trip cancellation insurance and have never regretted that decision. To date I have never had a situation that caused me to miss a trip and have saved thousands of dollars by not purchasing the insurance. Trip cancellation coverage reimburses you for prepaid, nonrefundable travel expenses due to illness or injury, whether it be you, a traveling companion, or a close family member that falls ill or becomes injured prior to departure. Sometimes this insurance also covers cancellations due to inclement weather, jury duty, natural disasters, or even terrorism. Depending upon how often you travel, skipping the added cost of trip cancellation insurance (typically 4–10 percent of the cost of your trip) more than pays for the possibility of losing what money you spent on a canceled trip.

I travel so often and do it at such a low cost that purchasing this type of coverage does not make sense for me. However, if you spend a lot of money up front when planning a vacation, this coverage may make sense for you. If losing that amount of money would hurt more than the peace of mind offered from purchasing coverage to protect the amount you invested in a trip, feel free to buy it. You have to make that decision for yourself. Maybe the word "scam" is a little harsh, but the online travel agencies have created a profitable upsell for themselves, and they definitely play on the fear of loss factor when customers book flights and hotels through their sites.

The good news is that online travel agencies such as Expedia or TripAdvisor negotiate on your behalf when it comes to getting a refund on hotels or tours in the event that you need to cancel your trip. Sometimes they can convince a vendor to turn a nonrefundable purchase into a refundable purchase, and sometimes they cannot. I have been successful more often than not in such instances. You won't know if you don't ask.

Trip cancellation insurance vs. trip interruption insurance

The major difference between trip cancellation insurance and trip interruption insurance is that trip cancellation insurance kicks in if something happens *before* you leave on your trip, while trip interruption insurance kicks in if something happens *after* you leave on your trip. As mentioned in the paragraph above, trip cancellation insurance covers prepaid, nonrefundable travel expenses from the time you make the purchase to the time you leave on your trip. These expenses may include flights, hotels, tours, pre-booked ground transportation, etc. Trip interruption insurance takes effect the moment you leave and expires when you arrive home. It covers the cost of getting you home early if you become injured or ill.

Cancellations, change fees, and refunds

Flights are usually the most difficult and expensive to change or cancel. Next comes hotels, followed by tours. Flights usually require a change fee of at least $150 if you are the one who initiates the change. To avoid this fee, always wait until the last minute to cancel or change a flight. There is a small chance the flight will be canceled by the airline because of weather, not having enough seats booked, or any other number of reasons. If the airline cancels the flight, you can avoid the change fee altogether. On very rare occasions, airlines will waive the change fee and issue a credit when you are the one who initiates the change, but I have only experienced this once or twice. It doesn't hurt to call the airline and try because asking will sometimes make up for it in an additional flight credit; however, it is best to assume that the $150 change fee is going to be a constant.

If you want to protect yourself against footing the bill for a hotel or tour in the case of a cancellation, you need to do so at the time of booking. Online travel agencies clearly delineate the cancellation terms for both hotels and tours. Most hotels are refundable up until a few days before the reservation date and most tours are refundable up until twenty-four hours before the date of the tour. If you wish to avoid the cost of trip cancellation insurance, avoid booking hotels and tours that state that they are nonrefundable. Then, the only loss you will have to incur from a canceled trip is the $150 change fee for each flight you booked.

During the coronavirus outbreak, I had to cancel a multi-country trip due to travel restrictions designed to prevent the spread of the disease. I had just finished booking all the tours and had to cancel them not long after I booked them. I waited until the last minute to cancel my flights, hoping the airlines would cancel the flight due to government travel restrictions. The airlines all ended up doing so, and I received a refund on all the flights, albeit many months later in some instances. Some of the hotels I had booked temporarily closed due to restrictions imposed by the local government. I received refunds for all of them (even those which stated that reservations were nonrefundable) due to the special circumstances.

CHAPTER 17

TRAVEL HEALTH INSURANCE

If you have an existing health insurance policy, you can rest assured knowing that most health insurance plans cover you for emergency health issues while traveling abroad for shorter trips. My health insurance carrier defines an international health emergency as any situation in which you risk losing your life or a limb if you do not get immediate medical care. This refers to anything that puts your life in serious danger or impairs how your body functions, such as losing a finger or having a stroke. They also consider seriously disfiguring yourself an emergency, which includes breaking your nose or having second-degree burns. Check your existing health insurance to see what is covered and what is not. Keep in mind that just because you may be covered by an out-of-network emergency room visit does not always mean it will be free. You may have to pay for some or all of the bill depending upon the details of your plan. In the case that you have to pay some or all of the bill, the expense will usually count toward your deductible or annual out-of-pocket maximum.

Accidental death and dismemberment insurance is usually offered free by your Visa or Mastercard. However, these companies will only cover you if you booked the trip using their specific card. Call your credit card company or check your card agreement for details. Visa Signature credit cards offer up to $100,000 and even sometimes as much as $250,000 in the event of your death, losing a limb, hand, foot, sight, speech, or hearing.

Some countries will ask you to provide proof of health insurance as an entry requirement as to avoid the financial burden of medical bills left unpaid by a tourist. Countries such as Cuba offer temporary health insurance at the airport for a nominal fee. Saudi Arabia requires visitors to purchase insurance as part of the online visa application process. If you are traveling for an extended period of time, such as studying abroad, engaging in an internship, participating in a gap year, or simply trying out the expat life, the rules are a little different. Some countries will dictate how much coverage you need if you are staying for an extended period of time. For example, the twenty-six countries in the Schengen area in Europe require travelers to obtain health insurance after their ninety-day tourist visa period expires. Factors that determine the cost of the insurance are insurance limits and deductibles, age of the traveler, and duration of your stay in a particular country or region. For a great comprehensive article on the different types of medical insurance offered, go to https://www.internationaltravelsecrets.com/travel-tools.

CHAPTER 18

FOREIGN LANGUAGE SECRETS

Luckily, there are very few places on Earth where people do not speak some semblance of English. Usually your waiter, hotel clerk, taxi driver, etc. can call one of their coworkers over to translate or answer your questions. While this applies mostly to touristy locations, I have been surprised by the number of people I have found off the beaten path who can communicate in English at least at a rudimentary level. This will not be the case in some Central Asian countries such as the -Stans. Many of those countries were part of the USSR, so unless you are up on your Russian, you will be out of luck. In many parts of West and North Africa, the locals speak French instead of English as there are many former French colonies in the region. I have even had some difficulties communicating in some parts of China and Korea. So what do you do when you are in a situation in which you cannot find anyone who speaks English?

Enter Google . . . again. Google Translate is an app I use often when traveling to these areas. You can type or copy and paste text into the app, and it will translate it into one of over a hundred different languages. Ever sat in a restaurant only to look at a menu in a language you have never even heard of? This is especially difficult if the menu has no photos of the dishes. Google Translate has a function which accesses the camera on your phone, and if you hover your phone over the text of the menu (or sign, or map, or newspaper—you get the idea), the words are transformed into English. The translation isn't always perfect, but you will get the gist fairly easily. Additionally, the conversation function allows you to speak into your phone, and your phone will translate your sentence into audio and text for the person you are speaking to. I use this with cab drivers, waiters, retail staff, etc. Never again do you have to worry about not knowing the language in a particular country or region.

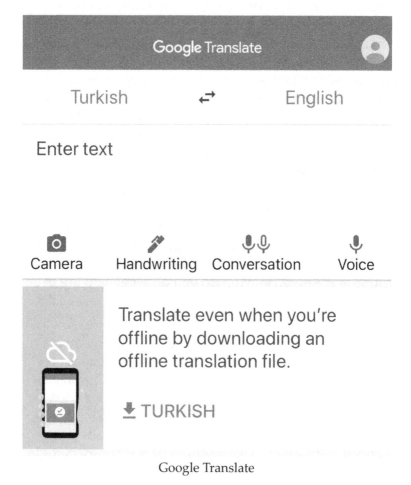

Google Translate

CHAPTER 19

RANDOM TIPS

Traveling abroad involves more than arranging and booking your tours, flights, accommodations, and means of transportation; navigating the currency and needed documents; and planning your stay. These additional tips will help you further enjoy your stay and your time in the airport.

TSA Precheck vs. Global entry vs. CLEAR

If you plan to travel internationally at all, go Global Entry all the way. Global Entry includes TSA Precheck, and it only costs an additional $15. TSA Precheck is $85 for five years and Global Entry is $100 for five years.

TSA Precheck allows you to keep your jacket, shoes, and belt on while you go through security in US airports. You also do not have to remove your laptop from your carry-on. The TSA website boasts that 95 percent of travelers wait less than five minutes in line. It takes just a few minutes to fill out an online application. You must then schedule a ten-minute, in-person appointment at a local enrollment center for a background check and fingerprinting. Once approved you will be issued a Known Traveler Number (or KTN) which you will have to add when purchasing airline tickets. More than 200 airports and seventy-three airlines provide TSA Precheck. Some airlines will automatically add it to your ticket if you have a frequent flyer account with them and you book directly through the airline website, not through a third-party site such as Expedia. Also, check to see if any of your credit cards have TSA Precheck benefits. For applications, appointments, or more info, go to https://www.tsa.gov/precheck

Global Entry not only includes TSA Precheck but it also speeds up the customs process upon returning to the US on an international flight. Global Entry allows travelers to use automatic kiosks to scan their passports, scan their fingerprints, and complete a customs declaration of what they brought back from their trips. After doing so, travelers receive a printed slip and are directed to the baggage claim and/or airport exit. For more information, go to https://www.cbp.gov/travel/trusted-traveler-programs/global-entry

CLEAR, unlike TSA Precheck and Global Entry, is not a government program. It is a private company out of New York that places scanners in the country's busiest airports and even large event venues such as the Staples Center. CLEAR kiosks scan your fingerprints and eyes allowing you to go directly to the front of the security line at airports. The downside is that the cost is $179 annually as opposed to the five years that the fees of TSA Precheck and Global Entry cover.

Negotiating

Do not be afraid to negotiate taxi fares and souvenir prices. Many cultures won't lend you respect if you don't at least try to negotiate. As with any negotiation, know in advance what your spending limit is or what you are willing to pay for something before you begin. Do not be afraid to walk away. If a shopkeeper or taxi driver keeps following you after you walk away, you are in their ballpark. Be firm yet polite. Also, know your currency conversions. We once walked around for twenty minutes trying to find a cab for 1,000 of the local currency rather than the inflated tourist price of 2,000. After doing the calculation, we realized that we only saved ourselves $1 which was not worth the time or the hassle.

When it comes to souvenirs, have a price that you are willing to pay in your mind before you begin the negotiation process. As with taxis, you may need to walk away in order to get a shopkeeper to come down to your desired price. You can always return and offer a higher bid if you really want to purchase the item in question. Personally, I avoid buying souvenirs as they tend to be pieces of junk that end up collecting dust in the garage. I only buy souvenirs that I get tangible use out of. I enjoy using the loose leaf teapot I purchased in Azerbaijan, the hand-painted cigar ashtray from Morocco, or the many t-shirts I have purchased from various locations around the world.

Best times of year to travel

By far the best times to travel are spring and fall. Not only is the weather milder, but destinations are less crowded and prices are lower. I try to avoid summer travel whenever possible since most people travel at that time because their kids are out of school. This causes tours and hotels to be sold out, resulting in a significant increase in price. For example, looking up a hotel in Prague, I see that the nightly rate is as high as $81 in July and almost half that price at $47 in May. Flights are also inflated: a one-way flight from Los Angeles to Prague is as much as $570 in July but is 60 percent less at $229 in May. In the summer, you can find me at home basking in the AC while planning my next trip for the fall. If your job or family situation only allows for a summer vacation, by all means, do what you have to do. Taking a trip under those circumstances is better than taking no trip at all. Be sure to use the flight booking secrets in chapter 2.

Weather app on your phone

The weather app is a good tool to use to determine what kind of clothes to pack and even what days to take tours. If I have four or five stops on a trip, I program each city into the weather app for an idea of what to expect. Don't end up being stuck in a twenty-degree situation with only a light jacket (yes, this has happened to me).

Create a winning itinerary

Creating a winning itinerary consists of a lot more than simply knowing your flight times and hotel addresses. True, these are important forms of data, but you will want to create a much more in-depth version for yourself. I create an email draft or a Google doc as I build my trip so I can access my work from any computer. The alternative is to create your trip on a Google doc for those of you who are familiar with that application. I have recently begun to use this option more often.

Include these details in your itinerary as you build your next trip:

1. Flight information including airline, flight number, and flight times
2. Whether or not your bags are paid for on your flight
3. What visas/entry requirements are needed to enter the country you are visiting
4. Currency conversion (ex. 100 Romanian Leu = $22)
5. Transportation info (Uber, taxi, train) to your hotel including time and cost
6. Hotel info including hotel address and agency you booked through
7. Tours booked, including dates, times, and operator contact info

8. List of landmarks you want to see that are not on one of your tours

9. Restaurants you want to try

Of course, you can add on to this list, but these are the essentials. Be sure to print out a copy and have an electronic version available somewhere.

Email your itinerary to yourself

While I always print a copy of my itinerary and carry it with me, I always email a copy to myself and a family member at home in case I lose track of it during the course of a trip. This is your fail-safe in case you happen to lose your printed copy as now you can access your itinerary through your phone or a hotel computer. I also give a printed copy to my travel companion in case we get separated, so they know our flight times, hotel reservations, and all the pertinent info for the entire trip. Your itinerary should include all the information you need on your trip, not just flight and hotel information. See the section above for all the specifics.

Asset list, will, and life insurance

Before every trip, I send an updated asset list to my father in case something happens to me. That way he is not left searching or waiting for statements to arrive if I become incapacitated while traveling. I include bank names, account numbers, and balances for all my investments, checking accounts, savings accounts, retirement accounts, and business accounts.

Tailor the amount of information you include on the asset list to the comfort level you have with the person with whom you are sharing it. You may want to only use the last four digits of your account number or even omit account balances. It is a good idea to disclose the location of any valuables hidden at home such as gold, jewelry, cash, etc. I also notate insurance policies and any business arrangements I have, including the location of said contracts in my office at home. If you have any outstanding debt, credit accounts, or automatic payments, include those as well so they can be attended to without going past due. Be sure to indicate any person that owes you a substantial amount of money along with the repayment terms. Keep a running list on your computer and update it at least once per year. I have found that if I prepare for the worst, it keeps the worst away.

Having an updated will is a good idea for anyone at any time, not just those seeking adventure abroad. Most wills need to be notarized or have witnesses (who aren't beneficiaries) sign. Check your state's laws for specifics. You want to have a will so that your property does not go to probate, allowing the government to determine where your assets go.

While life insurance is not always necessary, it can be a good idea if you have children, family members dependent on your income, or debt you owe to family members or friends. This type of insurance is usually cheap and only goes up in cost with age, existing health concerns, and amount of coverage. I pay $100 per year for $100,000 in life insurance coverage. This will cover any debts I have if something is to happen to me while on the road.

Having thick skin

In order to travel internationally (or anywhere for that matter), you must have thick skin. If you are someone who freaks out at the small things, international travel may not be your particular brand of vodka. In a word, things do not—no, things will not—always go as planned. Flights get canceled, hotels lose your booking, tour guides don't show up, phones die, credit cards get declined, and so on.

Also, remember that standards in other countries are much different from standards in the US. Do not expect waiters or cooks to be in any kind of hurry in restaurants—*ever*. Also do not be surprised if your silverware is not clean. Do not even get me started with restrooms. Some restrooms will have the foulest stench you have ever experienced, making you want to hold it for several hours before getting back to your hotel. Even your hotel may have some less than desirable accommodations. Do not be surprised if the AC isn't working or you have to take frigid cold showers because there is no hot water that day. As I mentioned earlier in this book, hotel reviews can help you avoid some of these situations, but not all the time. Thus, learning to laugh at your circumstances will carry you far.

One significant difference you may notice is that living standards are different everywhere you go. I remember arriving at our hotel in Nepal and getting a room on the sixth floor. Normally the sixth floor would not be a problem. However, this hotel did not have an elevator. To make things worse, many parts of the world refer to what we would call the first floor as "floor zero." That means that we were actually on the seventh floor and had to carry the luggage we brought up seven flights. Do not even ask me if there was a bellhop. Once we got into our room, we noticed a six-inch gaping hole to the outside in our bathroom. Was I upset? Nope. We were still out of breath from the climb up the stairs and laughed as we took pictures of the hole. Later in the trip, I went down on a motorbike hyperextending my knee and pulling my hamstring. I couldn't walk for two days and had to hop up seven floors, which took about twenty minutes to complete. I could have let this ruin my trip, but I still value the picture of me in front of the Taj Mahal in a wheelchair.

Another significant difference you will notice is that customer service representatives will not go out of their way for you. When checking in for a flight from Algeria to Senegal, the airline representative could not find our reservation. I showed her the confirmation email I received along with a separate email that contained a receipt proving that I had paid for the flight. The agent asked me if I had my credit card statement with me to prove that I had indeed paid for the flight. I responded by asking her if she routinely travels with her credit card statements. Her answer was no. As you can probably guess, we were required to purchase a new ticket at the inflated price despite the fact that I had already paid and received a confirmation. On top of that, we had to wait an additional five hours for our new flight. The airline employee was neither helpful nor sympathetic. In fact, she was condescending and accusatory.

I could have thrown a fit, but that would not have changed the circumstances. Getting angry not only causes the airline to not want to help you at all, but it also hinders your ability to think creatively to overcome the challenge at hand. By keeping my mind free of anger, I was able to find a flight five hours later with a different airline which was less than half of the full fare of purchasing a new ticket for our original flight. I was also able to get a refund for the flight we already paid for by calling the credit card company and disputing the charge. We took advantage of the extra five hours by returning to the city for food and drinks to pass the time.

It is more common for some of the smaller foreign airlines to cancel flights at the last minute. This can be frustrating if you have a connecting flight with another airline. We had a scheduled flight from Trinidad to Aruba with a stopover in Curaçao. Our flight from Trinidad to Curaçao was canceled at the last minute, which caused us to miss our connection with service to Aruba with another carrier. The airline did nothing to compensate us for our missed connection, no credit, discount, bag of peanuts, paper napkin, toothpick . . . nothing. It is what it is, and you have to be ready for these types of occurrences when you travel. They are unavoidable, so grin and bear it.

Dating abroad

Meeting locals or other travelers can add to the entire experience for those of you who are single. A word of caution here: I never choose to visit a location for the sole purpose of dating. If the opportunity presents itself, I see it only as a way to augment my experience in a particular destination. If you make dating your priority for traveling, you will be disappointed and it will taint your opinion of a country or city because of a bad experience. I make it a rule to never take a trip just to meet someone I have dated in the past while traveling as I have seen many friends get canceled on at the last minute after spending thousands on airline tickets and hotels. If I travel to meet up with someone I have dated in the past, I plan the trip as if no one else will be coming. That way I have a good time regardless of the outcome.

The social rules are different in every country, so be sure to do your research before you arrive. Be sure to be respectful when dating in other places by paying attention to local PDA rules and not being too aggressive. When in doubt, ask what is acceptable or not. They are more than willing to share with you what is typical in their cultures for dating situations. Some countries forbid single men to approach single women in public, while other countries allow women to be forward and even aggressive in approaching single men. It is good to know what kind of place you are visiting so you do not cause a scene or miss an opportunity to meet someone.

That said, let us discuss some tactics for meeting locals and other travelers. Restaurants, bars, and even public squares and parks are great places to spark up conversations with locals and other travelers in countries where cultural rules allow. Be aware of how people interact in a country. Some people in the world are more stoic; therefore, it may seem at first as if a person you are engaging with is not interested. Do not be afraid to ask directly for a coffee, drink, or dinner date to discover for certain whether or not someone is immune to your charms. It is easy to misinterpret cultural norms. I noticed that many of the people in Prague come off as stoic and uninterested, but if you approach them, they will respond. It just takes them a bit to warm up to you.

One way to be sure not only if someone is looking but also if someone is interested in you is online dating apps. While I despise using Tinder in the US, it is a helpful tool while traveling. Be sure to spend at least fifteen to twenty minutes swiping on those you like as soon as you can after arriving in a place because it can take several hours to several days to find a match, begin communication, and set up a date. If you prefer to handle this part of the dance before you even leave on your trip, use the upgraded form of Tinder to set your location to the destination you will be visiting. You can have several dates set up before you even arrive. The Bumble app works as well; however, it is not as prominent in most locations as Tinder.

Guys need to watch out for working girls. They are usually easy to spot on dating apps since they will be more scantily clad than most of the other girls. If you are not able to spot them on your own, don't worry. They will get down to the point quickly once you begin messaging them as they do not want to waste their time. Many locations around the world have large numbers of women engaged in the world's oldest profession, but I have seen the highest concentration in Asia and South America. Be wary of aggressive women who approach you at night as they won't always be dressed in the typical "uniform." Some will wear jeans and blend in with everyone else until the conversation starts. They, too, will usually make their intentions known after a short time. This is not my game of choice, but for those of you interested in "purchased" dates, the going rate is usually $25 to $100, depending upon the location. Many will quote a price as you walk by them. Some will even follow you for a while until you convince them that you are not interested. I advise against paid transactions as I have heard tales of tourists being robbed in their rooms. Dating in most locations is too easy to take the risk on a working girl anyway.

That said, I have had some great experiences dating locals across the globe. They tend to appreciate you more and will treat you very well. Some say it's because they know they have a limited time with you, but I believe it's simply the culture. We have such a dating culture at home of game playing that we have all become standoffish until things reach a certain point in a relationship. People across the world will tell you how they feel about you rather than wait until the "appropriate" time when it is "safe" to do so. In many cultures, it is common to wear their hearts on their sleeves. Most likely, you will even find yourself acting differently than you would at home. You will feel more open and the desire to reciprocate won't be based on any pre-planned chess moves or the advice of your crazy friends.

You may be surprised that one of my most memorable dates was about as PG as it gets. I approached the hostess of a seafood restaurant in Cartagena. She was a beautiful twenty-eight-year-old born in Colombia. I had taken this trip with a group of twenty friends, most of whom were drunk and obnoxious by the time dinner rolled around. This made her understandingly apprehensive when I approached her and went to work with my best Spanish (no doubt with an atrocious accent and horrible grammar). Luckily, one of my clients happened to call me while I was conversing with the hostess. I asked her to speak Spanish to the hostess and tell her that she should meet me after work. I handed the phone to the hostess and they talked for at least ten minutes. The hostess finally agreed. We walked to the beach and up the wall of a fort and talked for a few hours while sitting on a 500-year-old cannon that helped protect the city from pirates in the past. I had such a great time getting to know her and learning about how she grew up. She was a great person, and I still message her to this day. At about 10 p.m., her mother called her and asked why she was out so late. We said our goodbyes and she jumped on a bicycle to hurry home. The following evening, I pulled a passionate all-nighter with another local I met at a bar. That encounter was not nearly as memorable as the first. The point is that you never know what you are going to get. Sometimes you will meet someone you will want to go visit again. I have also met some that have come to visit me in the US.

Proposing to our waitress in Galapagos

TripAdvisor for restaurants

Since Yelp does not work in most other countries, the
TripAdvisor app is a formidable alternative. It shows
you all of the restaurants in your area, and you can
filter them by cuisine. Ratings from other customers
can help determine food quality, restaurant cleanliness,

service, etc. Since you never know what you are going to get in some locations, the photos of the interior and some of the more popular dishes are a great way to decide not only where to eat but also what to eat once you get there. TripAdvisor also allows you to browse categories based on price such as Fine Dining, Moderately Priced, and Cheap Eats. Or you can browse by meal (breakfast, brunch, lunch, coffee, dinner, bars & pubs, and dessert). Be sure to check out the "Local Cuisine" category if you want to avoid tourist trap pizza or hamburger joints that offer food that doesn't remotely resemble pizza or hamburgers.

CHAPTER 20

FAVORITE DESTINATIONS & RECOMMENDATIONS

To date, I have visited a total of ninety-nine countries. According to the UN, there are 195 countries in the world, 201 if you count states with limited recognition including Abkhazia, Kosovo, Northern Cyprus, South Ossetia, and Western Sahara. I do not know if I will get a chance to see them all, but I plan on seeing as many as I can. Here is a list of the countries I have visited in the order in which I experienced them:

USA	Slovakia	Ethiopia	Cyprus
Mexico	Hungary	Kenya	Kyrgyzstan
Canada	Russia	Tanzania	Mongolia
Greece	France	Panama	Tajikistan
Italy	Switzerland	Colombia	Azerbaijan
Vatican City	Portugal	Singapore	Uzbekistan
Spain	Morocco	Brunei	Trinidad and Tobago
Netherlands	Tunisia	Hong Kong*	Curaçao
Brazil	Grand Cayman	Norway	Aruba
Argentina	Cuba	Latvia	Dominican Republic
Peru	El Salvador	Czechia	Luxembourg
China	Costa Rica	Ireland	Ecuador
Vietnam	Guatemala	Iceland	Paraguay

Korea	Honduras	Belgium	Chile
Japan	UAE	Poland	Bolivia
Thailand	Maldives	Belarus	Israel
Laos	Sri Lanka	Ukraine	Georgia
Taiwan	Indonesia	Lithuania	Algeria
Philippines	Australia	Denmark	Senegal
Malaysia	New Zealand	England	Ivory Coast
Burma	Fiji	Cambodia	Slovenia
India	Belize	Nepal	Bosnia
Qatar	Germany	Kazakhstan	Oman
Turkey	Jordan	Romania	Saudi Arabia
Austria	Egypt	Serbia	

While Hong Kong is not one of the 195 countries recognized by the UN, it does have its own currency, parliamentary system, and passport and immigration system. It is officially deemed a "special administrative region" that has a loose affiliation with China and will continue to maintain its country-like status until 2047, when China will officially absorb it into its economic and legal system

Favorite destinations & recommendations

Below is a collection of some of my favorite places. Not sure where you should visit first? Take a free quiz to find out at https://www.internationaltravelsecrets.com/travel-tools.

BOLIVIA—This forgotten country is slightly off the beaten path compared to its more well-traveled neighbors. At just about 12,000 feet, the altitude can take some getting used to. But if you are looking for something outside the more popular Rio de Janeiro, Machu Picchu, or Buenos Aires, Bolivia is the place to be. This unique country boasts the Andes Mountains, the Amazon rainforest, and even Lake Titicaca. La Paz, one of the country's two capitals, is nestled in between these three geographic features.

The people are warm and visibly different from those of the surrounding countries. Many of the locals still don traditional garb. We were lucky enough to have a knowledgeable tour guide, an American who had married a local and gained Bolivian citizenship. He took us to see a different side of Bolivia that is not part of any normal tour and is far off the main road. We traveled up into the snowcapped Andes Mountains to an elevation of 15,000 feet, and even hiked at the edge of the Amazon forest. One of our stops was an abandoned hacienda with rooms we could explore, a beautiful courtyard, and the ruins of a church. He made a fire from scratch in the courtyard and cooked sausages in a pan of simmering beer. While he cooked lunch for us, we sipped wine and chewed coca leaves.

Chewing coca leaves is common in several South American countries. It is also common to find coca tea, coca beer, and sometimes even coca candy. While these items are made from the coca leaf, they are indeed all natural and not harmful. The leaf actually has several health benefits including easing the effects of altitude sickness, encouraging feelings of euphoria, alleviating pain, reducing hunger, and creating an energy boost. It is impossible to overdose on the natural form of the leaf which includes chewing the leaf or drinking tea. Cocaine, however, is the concentrated form of extracts from the leaf and can be harmful and addictive. Colombia mistakenly has the reputation for cocaine, but that is simply because it was widely distributed thanks to Pablo Escobar. The drug is most commonly produced in Bolivia, and Escobar simply purchased it here and distributed it in Colombia. Ahh, traveling is educational, isn't it?

GEORGIA—The Republic of Georgia is another unknown gem in Central Asia. It sits with Russia to the north, the Black Sea to the east, and borders Turkey, Armenia, and Azerbaijan to the south. This country is the perfect blend of Eastern Europe and Central Asia. The Russian influence is much heavier in Georgia than it is in Azerbaijan as Georgia was conquered by Russia twice: once by the Russian Empire in 1801 and again by the USSR in 1921. There are even territorial disputes with Russia to this day.

The architecture and historical sites in this country will mesmerize you, and the food is some of the best I've had in all my travels. Georgian people are very proud of their wine, and they will tell you that wine first originated here. And yes while evidence of wine was found in Georgia dating back to 6000 BC, China has evidence of a fermented grape and rice mixture about a thousand years earlier. Either way, Georgian wine has a unique flavor. While it was not my favorite wine of all time, I did make it a point to partake at most meals while visiting. I even got to try Stalin's favorite wine. Stalin was born in Georgia, and you can even visit his birthplace. I boarded his train car that he used to travel to the conferences at Yalta and Potsdam (Stalin did not like to fly). I saw where he slept and even was able to touch the conference table at which he sat with his top aides. We also got to visit the Uplistsikhe cave town with its ornately carved ceilings and fascinating history. Be sure to take the tour that covers Stalin's hometown, Uplistsikhe Cave Town, and the Jvari Monastery all in one day. Overall, I like the vibe in this country and could definitely spend more time here.

COLOMBIA—If you ever get the chance to visit Colombia, I recommend you stay in the walled city in Cartagena. The walled city is the safer part of Cartagena, even at night. The city is right on the Caribbean Sea and has a variety of restaurants and bars with good food, drinks, and ambiance. The KGB Bar is unique as it is littered with KGB paraphernalia including uniformed mannequins and propaganda posters. Catty-corner to the KGB Bar is a Cuban cigar bar that boasts live Cuban music, Cuban cigars, and mojitos. Not far down the street are two great restaurants—La Cevicheria and Marzola Parilla Argentina. La Cevicheria has some excellent seafood dishes (and a beautiful hostess named Angelly). Marzola Parilla Argentina has a delectable meat selection and an impressive Argentinian wine list. The history in the walled city is definitely not lacking either. In fact, you can see a dent in a church that actually came from a cannonball shot from Sir Francis Drake's ship.

AZERBAIJAN—This is by far one of my favorite destinations. I had never even heard of this country until I slowly began to use up my "new country" pass and had to find somewhere that I had not yet visited. Enter Azerbaijan. This former USSR country borders Russia to the north and Iran to the south. It is on the exact opposite side of the globe from the US, and it definitely feels like it when you arrive. Its unique blend of Russian, Persian, and Central Asian cultures reveals itself in the food, architecture, religion, and culture as a whole. If you get the chance to visit this gem, stay in the Old City in Baku. Nestled on the coast of the Caspian Sea, the old city has restaurants and shops that some say have continuously been shops since the seventh century. This city is very safe and clean compared to some of its Central Asian neighbors. Be sure to visit a hammam if you get the chance. This is an ancient Azerbaijani tradition that mimics the experience of a spa, but not really. You do get to sit in saunas, relax in hot and cold pools, and even enjoy a massage, but hammams offer unique services I have not found anywhere else outside the region. One is getting beat by oak leaf branches. Next is getting an abrasive body scrub that leaves your skin tingling. You may even be massaged with coffee, honey, and salt. The salt increases circulation while the honey and coffee have healing properties that reduce inflammation.

LAOS—This forgotten country is still relatively untouched by Western tourists but probably won't be for long. Flights to the capital city, Vientiane, are a bit expensive at more than $750 from the US with two or more layovers—unless you do a little research. Your best bet is to get a flight to Hanoi, Vietnam, for as low as $350 and catch a flight to Laos for $98 (total flight cost $448). Another option is to get a flight to Bangkok, Thailand, for as low as $383 and a flight to Laos for $70; or Kuala Lumpur, Malaysia, for as little as $415, and a flight to Laos for $38 (total flight cost $453 for either option).

Once you find your path to this out-of-the-way place, many adventures await you. The capital, Vientiane, has so many sights ranging from golden stupas to the Victory Gate (their version of the Arc de Triomphe) to the beautiful Buddha Gardens. Vang Vieng is a city in the mountains in which you can see wild water buffalo float by in a nearby river with breathtaking mountain views behind it. This is a majestic spot all but untouched by tourists, so it is a good place to relax and reflect. There is a kickin' party scene further up the river and in parts of town if that's your thing, but those spots can be easily avoided if you so desire. Accommodations right on the river go for $20 per night if you look in the right spots.

ISTANBUL—I have been to Istanbul more than any other city in the world. The only city that comes close as far as number of visits is Paris, and the only reason is that CDG Airport is one of the cheapest hubs to fly into with flights as low as $197, but I digress. One of the more intriguing features of Istanbul is that it stands as a gate between East and West. I'm not just talking about culture—half of the city literally sits in Europe, and the other in Asia. Istanbul is separated by the Bosphorus Strait, which connects the Black Sea to the Sea of Marmara, thus separating the two continents. The city definitely shows signs of that clash. You will find hints of Persia, Central Asia, and Eastern Europe in the history, culture, food, and architecture. You will see walls built by Emperor Constantine, towers built by the Genoese, and an Eastern Orthodox Church built by Emperor Justinian.

If you fly into SAW Airport, you will land on the Asia side and can grab a cab or an Uber to the city center on the European side for a ride that takes about forty-five minutes. If you are looking for some variety and great photo opportunities, take a taxi from SAW to the ferry terminal and take a ferry across the Bosphorus Strait. You will see mosques on the skyline along with other unique landmarks. If you fly into the new IST airport, you will land on the European side of the city and it will now take you about forty-five minutes to get to the city center. The IST Airport used to be much closer (about twenty minutes closer) but was moved to another location in 2019 in order to accommodate a larger number of passengers.

The Hagia Sophia is a great place to visit. It was constructed in 532 AD and originally served as an Eastern Orthodox Church and was the largest cathedral in the world for almost a millennium. It became a Mosque when the Ottomans invaded in the fifteenth century and remained so until it was turned into a museum in the 1930s. The mosaics and Christian and Muslim art make this wonder of architecture more enticing as a must-see.

Galata Tower is another prominent landmark that

decorates the Istanbul skyline. The tower itself was built in 1308 by the Genoese and was originally used as a way to spot fires in the city as well as to watch for enemy ships. Now a restaurant (Galata Kule Restoran) and supposedly a nightclub occupy the top floors. The area around the tower contains many restaurants and shops worth exploring.

Sensus Food & Wine is located close to Galata Tower and boasts a host of Turkish wine and a great selection of cheeses, meats, and sausages. The waiters are knowledgeable and friendly. I had the pleasure of trying a cabernet sauvignon/cabernet franc blend by Selendi Sarnic. Try it and you won't regret it. Also order the Özel Seçilen Soğuk Etler, which is a cold meat plate consisting of beef bacon, Bosnian dried meat, and Italian salami.

Gulhane Sur Cafe is located near the Hagia Sophia and is on a hill on a charming cobblestone street, but that is not what makes it unique. It is a terraced outdoor cafe whose back wall is a structure built 600 years ago by the Ottoman Turks. Here you can smoke hookah (shisha) while enjoying Turkish coffee, Arabic tea, and a selection of small bites — a great place to take a break and watch the city go by.

You can get to Istanbul for as little as $418, depending upon your departure city with at least one stop. However, if you are planning a trip to Eastern Europe or the Middle East, you can visit Istanbul for free as many flights to the region have a long layover in this beautiful city.

CHAPTER 21

UNFORGETTABLE MOMENTS

So many amazing things can happen when traveling—
serendipitous moments that touch your soul, create
memories, or forge life-long friendships.

Couple from Algeria

One such unexpected moment came when I met a
young married couple in their twenties while smoking
hookah on a layover in Istanbul. They were from Algeria
and invited me to come see their home country. I took
them up on their offer as I luckily already had a trip
planned to Algeria a few months later. They invited
me into their home, made us a home-cooked meal,
and acted as our tour guides for several days. They
were so warm and welcoming. The husband owned
and operated a clothing store, and the wife was a
newscaster. Despite this fact, they both took time off
whenever they could to show us around, and we have
remained friends ever since.

Algerian couple I met on a layover in Istanbul

Enjoying dessert in their home in Algiers, Algeria

Early Morning in Kyrgyzstan

On an around-the-world trip, we had just flown into Kyrgyzstan from Cyprus for a quick stop on our way to Mongolia. We had stayed up late and partied all night in Cyprus since our flight was not set to land in Kyrgyzstan until 7 a.m. When we arrived at our hotel, I went straight to bed since I was so exhausted. After about ten minutes I noticed that my friend had not entered the room yet, so I looked out the door to our room to see what was holding him up. Our door opened up into a beautiful courtyard with a table in the middle. My friend was sitting at the table with seven guys from Saudi Arabia and waved me over. The men, wearing traditional robes, invited us to share some delicious Arabic tea and some fresh dates they had brought in from their hometown. We drank and chatted with them for over an hour, creating another unforgettable memory. Upon returning to our room, my friend remarked how he could not believe we had seen a Pearl Jam concert in Amsterdam, watched a seventy-year-old man do the splits on a dancefloor in Cyprus, and drank tea with seven guys from Saudi Arabia all in a matter of days.

One of our new friends from Saudi Arabia

Adventures in Honduras

While visiting Copan, a small mountain town in Honduras, we met a small group of PhD students from various countries in Central America. When the bar closed sometime after midnight, we all relocated to a park just outside the bar. One of the PhD students pulled a bottle of vodka from her backpack, and we passed the bottle around as we talked. It began to rain heavily, but we stayed and drank anyway. My friend had so many drinks that he began jumping in rain puddles. Though I was still respectably sober, I couldn't figure out why my friend was so drunk as he can always outdrink me. I discovered the reason when I pulled the handwritten bar receipt out of my pocket the next morning. He and I both had ten drinks at the bar. Next to my friend's drinks, the receipt said "dobles," which means doubles in Spanish. Essentially my friend had the equivalent of twenty drinks *before* we went out and started taking swigs out of the vodka bottle.

Needless to say, he had a hangover the next day. I fixed him right up with a full breakfast of fresh eggs, sausage, ham, salsa, and tortillas along with freshly squeezed orange juice and coffee. We ate on the patio of an old restaurant and watched horse-drawn carts go by on cobblestone streets. No better way to nurse a hangover.

We hired a driver and guide to take us from Vientiane to Vang Vieng in Laos. It was a six-hour drive on an unpaved road. On the way, the guide asked us if we wanted to see the Buddha caves. Sure? He pulled off the main road and drove on a sketchy path for about ten minutes. We stopped on a narrow mountain path, and the guide told us to exit the van and follow him around a curve on the path. Meanwhile, the driver started to turn around and drive away. I seriously thought we were going to die and they were going to take off with our luggage. I told my friend I was going to stay with the van and told him to go with the guide to look at what was behind the corner, but not to leave my line of sight. When he looked around the corner, he yelled, "OH MY GAWD!!!" Sure enough, there were caves with Buddha figures carved into the side of them. We took pictures and got back on the road to Vang Vieng.

Vang Vieng is a mountain village along a river with majestic views. We jumped into a kayak and watched an almost fully submerged herd of water buffalo pass us and continue under a stick bridge. This was one of the most peaceful places I had ever experienced. Further up the river is a strip of bars with water slides that dump you into the water. Bar goers have large inner tubes and go from bar to bar on the river. This faraway mountain town was the perfect mix of serenity and party.

Water buffalo in Vang Vieng, Laos

Brewery in Laos

After a few days here, our guide took us back to the capital city of Vientiane. He was kind enough to give us a city tour. On the tour, we stopped at the Beer Lao factory, where they make the only beer offered in the entire country of Laos that, like most of the beers of the world, tastes like a watered-down Heineken or Carlsberg. While waiting outside the entrance of the large brewery, we noticed our guide vehemently arguing with the guard at the gate as he pointed feverishly in our direction. The guard looked nervous and reluctantly let us pass. We asked our guide what had happened. To get us in, our guide had told the guard we were rich American investors and that if he did not open the gate and let us in, we were not going to invest in the facility. We could not stop laughing. We were then escorted into the warehouse with pallets of beer stacked taller than we were by almost two times. Our guide cracked open three twenty-two-ounce bottles of dark Beer Lao, and it was delicious. We asked him why we did not see the dark beer offered at any of the restaurants and bars. He informed us that the darker beer is their premium product, and since no one in the country can afford it, it is produced only for export.

Beer Lao Brewery in Laos

Lost passport in Tanzania

Once I lost my passport (well sort of) while traveling in Tanzania and didn't realize it until we were packing up to leave for the airport. The US consulate was closed until after the weekend, so our hotel arranged a ride for us to visit a local official in order to get a letter that would allow us to leave the country. I would deal with getting back into the US after we landed, but as long as I could *get* to Los Angeles, I knew I would be fine.

I walked into a building that had a wooden sign that read "No Corruption Zone." Little did I know the irony of the sign at the time of my arrival. I eventually found myself being questioned by a uniformed officer in a small office. He was not friendly at all and kept asking me why I lost my passport as if I had done it on purpose. After twenty minutes of questions, he asked me to follow him to the main boss upstairs who was wearing a communist suit much in the style of Mao Zedong or Kim Jong Un. I was warned on the way up the stairs to make my case in a concise yet subservient manner. I did so at first and worked up enough of a rapport with the boss that I went so far as to joke around with him a bit. This seemed to throw off the uniformed officer that had brought me upstairs. After a few minutes of chatting, the boss informed the officer to complete some paperwork downstairs and I was ushered out of the boss's office. The officer completed the paperwork and stood up to deliver it to the boss. Unsure, I asked him if I needed to go with him. He stopped and thought for a moment and motioned to me. "Bring your tongue," he said with a slight grin on his face as I must have impressed him with how I handled his boss. After getting the paperwork approved, I was once again led out of the boss's office. The uniformed officer gave me a play-by-play on how to obtain the letter I needed to leave the country: I was to go to a nearby bank and obtain a clean crisp new US $100 bill, then offer it to the boss underneath my paperwork in a nonchalant, indirect way as to not offend him. At that point, I would receive the signed letter from the boss. I did as I was told and got the letter I needed to leave the country. So much for the "no corruption zone," I guess.

I happened to be dating a girl at the time who worked for US National Security and had been sharing the comical situation with her via text as it unfolded. I did not discover this until later, but she had arranged for a replacement passport to be sent to customs in Los Angeles. The passport mishap caused us to miss our original flight home, including an attractive layover in Zanzibar in which we were going to have a few hours of beach time before taking the long flight home. We were able to catch a flight a few hours later with the same airline sans the layover in Zanzibar. The irony of the story was that as we were enjoying a few beers in the airport bar, I discovered my passport in the pocket of my backpack. I do not understand how it happened because I always place my passport in this same small pocket. I checked the pocket three times and my friend also checked it, and the passport wasn't there. It's impossible to miss, yet it appeared in the pocket at the airport bar. Maybe we weren't supposed to go to Zanzibar. Maybe something bad was going to happen. Maybe I am just a blind moron who overlooked the passport all along. I'll vote for the last explanation.

Vietnam travels

My first trip to Vietnam is what helped reignite the travel bug in me. We stopped at Nha Trang, a sleepy coastal town about 270 miles north of Saigon. We rented motorbikes and rode about forty-five minutes inland to one of the best spas I have experienced in my life. We started out by taking a mud bath in a large ceramic bowl meant to hold three Vietnamese people, so the three of us were squished since we are all over six feet tall. Next we took a tea bath, which was a still hot Jacuzzi in which they dipped a tea bag the size of a soccer ball. We were surrounded by beautiful vegetation and relaxing music. After the best ninety-minute massage I have ever received, we sat underneath a heated waterfall to decompress before taking leave of the spa.

We rode our motorbikes to the coast and got into what

resembled large wooden bowls that acted as boats. Each bowl held three people plus a villager who rowed us to floating docks about 200 feet offshore. The floating docks had vats containing different fish, shrimp, and lobster. We all picked out our own fish and lobsters and went back to a restaurant on the shore that cooked our fish and served it alongside all the fixings. A great meal to follow a great massage—one of the more memorable days while traveling.

Boat to the floating docks in Nha Trang

When we returned to Saigon, we stayed in a hotel directly across from a spa that offered mani-pedi services, haircuts, and massages. Our group spent a lot of time here because the massages were ninety minutes for about $7. When we arrived, a group of twenty girls lined up, and we got to choose whom we wanted to give us a massage. Don't worry—this isn't one of "those" massage places. They were actually very professional, and from what I understand, they came down pretty hard on anyone who offered "extra" services. I befriended one of them, and we met at a bar not far from the hotel. She took me to meet three of her friends at a local seafood restaurant. We sat outside on the street on little stools that were barely big enough for a kindergartener. I ordered some excellent seafood dishes and several buckets of beer. She shucked all the shellfish and hand-fed me as we drank into the wee hours of the night. When the restaurant closed and the check came, I offered to pay the entire bill. They fought me for it, but I had a good time eating and drinking with them and wanted to thank them. For a whole night of drinking and eating quality seafood, I do not think I have ever gotten such a bargain. Best twenty dollars I ever spent.

CHAPTER 22

TRAVEL AS FOOD FOR THE SOUL

Taking international trips allows for a time of self-reflection. Experiencing buildings that are over a thousand years old, or a landscape I thought only existed in fairytales often clears my head, allowing me to become more creative and think about what I may want to add to my experience at home. I often create a list of tasks to complete upon returning to the US. Some are tasks that have been on my mind for some time, and others pop up while on the road. I have added such things as playing guitar daily, buying and reading a new book, engaging in daily meditation, cooking at home more often, or meeting up with an old friend. Many of these pertain to living a full life. I tend to get in a rut when I am home for too long. I am less likely to notice the simple pleasures, such as a park down the street or a local museum that I have been saying I would visit for years. Upon returning home, I am still in that place of childlike wonder, and so I pay closer attention to things I pass by every day. I have admired hundred-year-old trees in my neighborhood that I have never noticed in the two decades I have lived in the city.

Coming home from an international trip has a way of clearing out the clutter in my mind and allowing me to hit the reset button. I become more productive and come out of the gate full speed when returning to work after a trip, crossing off self-improvement tasks as easily as work tasks. I often return home with creative ideas to address challenges or augment my business in some way. And what's more is that I have a lot more vigor and drive when implementing them. Work becomes fun again, and as a result, efficiency rises and income spikes. It is funny to note, though, that I get antsy after a few months and begin to feel drawn to travel to another place to start the process all over again. I consider myself lucky to have the ability to take four to five international trips per year. The nature of my work and the ability to find cheap fares and accommodations put me in a unique position. I hope that you are able to at least harvest some of the secrets I have included in this text and find a way around your work schedule to go out and experience the world in the ways I have — without spending your life savings.

Despite the fact that this book is about spending time thousands of miles away from home, I cannot convey enough how much I look forward to coming home at the end of a trip to sleep in my own bed, have that burger that I have been craving, and see loved ones again. Traveling makes me appreciate home on a much deeper level and see it in a completely different light.

"We shall not cease from exploration,
and the end of all our exploring
will be to arrive where we started
and know the place for the first time."

-T.S. Eliot

Thank You!

To thank you for taking the time to read my book, I am offering a free video to help you save some serious cash on your next trip!

FREE VIDEO
How to find destinations with the lowest airfare!

Learn how to find the cheapest places in the world to fly. Choose your next travel destination based on the lowest fares--anywhere in the world! Go to https://www.internationaltravelsecrets.com/free-video to get access to the video.

Now that you have gained some in-depth knowledge on international travel, I invite you to keep the adventure going. Need some help booking that next trip? I can help!

ONLINE COURSES

Let me show you step-by-step how to book cheap flights around the world, find hotels in the best places, and choose tours that fit your needs. These courses will take you deeper into the information presented in this book and hold your hand in the process, so you don't miss a step. Go to https://www.internationaltravelsecrets.com/online-courses.

TRIP PLANNING SERVICES

Stuck while trying to plan your next trip? Book a one-on-one consult to get the answers you need to finish booking your dream trip to spots all over the world. I am happy to assist. Go to https://www.internationaltravelsecrets.com/travel-with-me.

TRAVEL WITH ME - ORGANIZED GROUP TRIPS

Don't want to spend the time researching and planning your next trip? Let me do the work for you in organizing the best flights, hotels, landmarks, visa requirements, ground transportation, and everything else you need to complete before visiting that country on your bucket list. Join me and a small group of travelers to visit destinations around the world. All you have to do is show up. Go to https://www.internationaltravelsecrets.com/travel-with-me.

DON'T GO YET!

I NEED YOUR HELP!

I really appreciate your feedback and love hearing what you have to say. I need your input to make the next version of this book and my future books better.

Please leave me a helpful review on Amazon letting me know what you thought of the tips I shared with you.

Please also refer this book to anyone you know who can benefit from these travel secrets. Let's get more people traveling the world!

Thank you so much!

-Michael Wedaa